Graphic Inc. is committed to presenting exceptional work in international Design, Advertising, Illustration & Photography

Published by **Graphis** I Publisher&Creative Director: B. Martin Pedersen I Design: Yon Joo Choi, JiEun Lee, Gregory Michael Cerrato I Editorial: Ariel Davis I Production: Jennifer Berlingeri, Abigail Jemma Newman I Support Staff: Rita Jones I Design&Production Interns: Kristen Rego

Remarks: We extend our heartfelt thanks to contributors throughout the world who have made it possible to publish a wide and international spectrum of the best work in this field. Entry instructions for all Graphis Books may be requested from: Graphis Inc., 307 Fifth Avenue, Tenth Floor, New York, New York 10016. visit our web site at www.graphis.com

Anmerkungen: Unser Dank gilt den Einsendern aus aller Welt, die es uns ermöglicht haben, ein breites, internationales. Spektrum der besten Arbeiten zu veröffentlichen. Teilnahmebedingungen für die Graphis-Bücher sind erhältlich bei: Graphis, Inc., 307 Fifth Avenue, Tenth Floor, New York, New York 10016. Besuchen Sie uns im World Wide Web www.graphis.com

Remerciements: Nous remercions les participants du monde entier qui ont rendu possible la publication de cet ouvrage offrant un panorama complet des meilleurs travaux. Les modalités d'inscription peuvent être obtenues auprès de: Graphis, Inc., 307 Fifth Avenue, Tenth Floor, New York, New York 10016. Rendez-nous visite our notre site web: www.graphis.com

Contents

Previous spread: Image from EVERYTHING IN THE RIGHT PLACE by Bisgrafic | *Opposite page:* Image from Art Center College of Design Poster by Michael Schwab Studio

InMemoriam

John Alvin *1948~2008*

Kay Amert *1947~2008*

Richard Eckersley *1941~2006*

Carles Fontseré *1916~2007*

Tim Hildebrandt *1939~2006*

Alton Kelley *1940~2008*

Pierre Mendell *1929~2008*

Taku Satoh: Designing for Issey Miyake

What was the assignment you were given on this job and were there any limitations?

We were simply asked "To freely express the atmosphere of PLEATS PLEASE ISSEY MIYAKE" and there were no limitations as far as expression was concerned. Out of the four suggestions I presented to Issey Miyake, the Sushi series was chosen. The series of Sushi ads were inserted in the in-flight magazine of All Nippon Airways *Wingspan*. The Sushi series appeared four times throughout the year 2008. And was so well received that I decided to contact Issey Miyake's staff to suggest that we make posters out of this campaign.

Where did you get the inspiration for these exceptional posters?

The most important aspect was to see that Pleats Please has characteristics no other clothing line has. So many key words and phrases came from there. For example, it is compact, light, fun, bright, free, and one can pick from the various choices. In my mind, these words are linked together with sushi, the symbolic dish of the Japanese culture. If I were to liken Pleats Please to a creative tool, it would be either paint or clay. They are unconventional materials that allow you to express just about anything. Those thoughts were in my head ever since I started working for Issey Miyake four years ago.

Did you have the honor of working with Issey Miyake directly or did you work through other people on his staff?

I worked directly with him on almost all of our creations. Also, together with Mr. Naoto Fukasawa, Mr. Miyake and I work as directors at the 21_21 DESIGN SIGHT, which opened on March 2007 in Tokyo. Together, we plan exhibitions for this facility. My first encounter with Mr. Miyake was in 2003 at the A-POC exhibition held in Tokyo. In 2001, I had started a project of my own, analyzing mass-produced goods from the design point of view. I had been asked to analyze A-POC from the design point of view and I installed a room of "Anatomy" inside the A-POC exhibition. Then I created the "VI" for The Miyake Issey Foundation, worked on the design for the package renewal of his perfume L'eau D'Issey, and designed the catalogue for Pleats Please.

How was he to work with?

Mr. Issey Miyake is gifted with a keen sense of intuition. He receives inspiration from all areas and presents it to us. At first, his presented ideas and themes seemed to come from somewhere very far and they confused me. However, as the time passed, I felt myself awakening to those inspirations. It is an honored feeling to experience firsthand that the people around him and people from all over the world are inspired by his ideas.

You have designed extraordinary posters in the past. Is this one of your favorite mediums in design?

I work with all types of media and therefore don't create that many posters. These days where media is usually in an interactive form, I feel that a two-dimension poster has a power of its own. A motionless media can be full of grace, and it spells out determination. In a way, a designer's strength is tested in such a medium.

What motivates you most?

My motivation comes from being touched or moved by something. There is so much to explore in the world of nature and these wonders give me the power of motivation.

What part of your work do you find the most demanding?

I would not say which part exactly. I find all of my work challenging and interesting. I feel that it is entirely up to you whether to make your work interesting or not. I always try to find some elements that can shift my work to a more absorbing direction. It is same with themes such as ecology that tend to make creators think in a more serious way.

What personal goals have you set for yourself?

I do not have a final goal set for myself. I would like to always be able to experiment in unexplored territories.

What satisfies you most in your work?

I am never satisfied. I am always questioning my own work. That is because all of my previous works are works of the past to me now. I feel that if a creator is satisfied in their past work, he or she is doomed. Designs change with the activity of the human race. Therefore, with the world in such an unstable state, it is unnatural and dangerous to feel so secure and satisfied. I feel that it is healthy to feel insecure, and what we need is to change those feelings into our motivations.

Who do you admire in the profession, from the past and/or present, and why?

There are admirable people in all sorts of professions such as design, art, literature, music, architecture, life science, politics, etc. However, it is almost impossible to see their true selves from their works or actions and the irresponsible reports from the media. Before, I would have picked a few names, but now, I feel that the environment itself, including human beings, is a miracle and worth praising. The Japanese word Arigato meaning "thank you," came from a phrase, "Arigatai", literary meaning "rarely possible", which leads to the meaning "unbelievable" and "blissful". We have to thank our usual days that are "blissful" to all of us. I hope that each and every one of us can remember this. Thank you.

Taku Satoh was born in Tokyo in 1955. He completed his undergraduate studies from the Design Department of Tokyo National University of Fine Arts and Music in 1979 and his graduate studies in 1981 before joining Dentsu Inc. He established the Taku Satoh Design Office in 1984. He is well known for his designs of Nikka Pure Malt, Lotte Mint Gum Series, S&B Foods' Spice and Herb Series and MEIJI Dairies' Oishii Gyunyu. He has produced several publications, including "Analysis of the Mass product Design" series (Bijutsu Shuppan-sha), and "A whale was blowing water" (Transart). His exhibitions have included "Designs in Ordinary Lives" (2006) at Contemporary Art Gallery of Art Tower Mito, and Exhibition Directed by Taku Satoh "water" (2007) at 21_21 DESIGN SIGHT. His principal awards consist of the Mainichi Design Award, Tokyo ADC Award, and the Yusaku Kamekura Design Award.

Issey Miyake was born in Hiroshima in 1938 and graduated from the Tama Art University in Tokyo in 1964. After working in both Paris and New York City, he established the Miyake Design Studio in Tokyo in 1970. Three years later, he began showing his line at the Paris Collections, featuring the exploration of space between the human body and the cloth that covers it. PLEATS PLEASE ISSEY MIYAKE began in 1993 as a radical yet practical clothing line that combines technology and beauty by with a process called garment pleating. In 1998, the A Piece of Cloth (A-POC) project began, using a new computer technology to create clothing beginning with a single piece of thread. In 2004, Miyake established the Miyake Issey Foundation with the Ministry of Education and Science, which publishes literature and organizes exhibitions and events.

TOKYO == Place Minami-Aoyama 3-13-21 Minami-Aoyama, Minato-ku, Tokyo Phone : 03.5772.7750 ▪ PARIS == 201 Boulevard Saint Germain, 75007 Paris Phone : 01.45.48.10.44 == 3Bis Rue des Rosiers, 75004 Paris Phone : 01.40.29.99. 66 ▪ NEW YORK == 128 Wooster Street, New York, NY 10012 Phone : 212.226.3600 == tribeca ISSEY MIYAKE 119 Hudson Street, New York, NY 10013 Phone : 212.226.0100 ▪ LONDON == 20 Brook Street, London W1K 5DE Phone : 020.7495.2306

Darrin Alfred: Curator, Denver Art Museum

What are the criteria for a poster to be included in your collection?
There are numerous standards on which a decision may be based when considering a poster, or any graphic work, for acquisition. It has been essential for us to continually address our collection's strengths and weaknesses. The proposed poster must recognize and speak to these conditions in some measure or another. Additionally, I look for work I personally respond to on an emotional level and, most notably, the purpose of any poster is to attract the eye in the briefest of intervals. It is in this deceptively simple respect that the work must excel.

What do you think are the most important posters in your organization's collection? Why?
In February 2008, the Museum acquired a collection of approximately 875 psychedelic rock-concert posters from the mid-1960s through the early 1970s. Wildly experimental, these works reflect the psychedelic experience through a melting pot of hallucinatory imagery and unorthodox juxtapositions of electric colors. The artists who created some of the iconic images of the era—Victor Moscoso, Lee Conklin, and Rick Griffin—were influenced by Art Nouveau, Surrealism, and Josef Albers' color theory. The material, assembled by Colorado-based collector David Tippit, includes a complete first-print set of posters for the legendary promoter Bill Graham's Fillmore Auditorium concerts, plus posters for other San Francisco venues, including the Avalon Ballroom, Winterland, and the Matrix.

What is your favorite poster in the collection? What makes it so appealing?
Milton Glaser's 1967 image of Bob Dylan. Glaser's iconic poster of the young musician effectively captured the essence of how people felt about the singer-songwriter and his music at that time. Glaser portrayed Dylan as a black silhouette with a shock of kaleidoscope hair that perfectly expressed the times and the singer's counterculture message.

How does your poster collection stand out from poster collections worldwide?
Before my arrival in 2007, the Museum had been building one of the most important contemporary design collections in the United States. The department has, of course, continued to build upon the collection's existing strengths—which include noteworthy examples of contemporary typography, posters, and other combinations of text and image—with the intention of upholding our dedication to creating one of the most comprehensive and well thought-out holdings of American graphic design. The recent acquisition of the AIGA Design Archives was a major step towards this goal. In addition to the Museum's existing graphic design collection, it is the stewards of the AIGA Design Archives. The archive, which contains a significant number of posters, represents the most comprehensive holding of contemporary American graphic design in the world. This collection of more than 6,000 objects is augmented annually with a gift of about 300 award-winning items from the year's AIGA design competitions.

Are there any outstanding poster designers that have caught your eye recently?
Jason Munn. The man behind The Small Stakes moniker, Munn is a master of the simple, direct and artful concert poster. Influenced by advertising and poster art of the 1940s and 1950s (think Alvin Lustig, Saul Bass, and Paul Rand), and the music itself, Munn is an artist who responds to simplicity and clarity. His work is abstract, meticulous, and, although very modern, carries strong echoes of nineteenth-century posters and pamphlets from both the American West and the Victorian music hall. Munn's rich tactile graphics, great use of negative space, and beautifully minimal typography prove that he is a textbook example of the "less is more" philosophy. While his techniques vary from piece to piece, there is a strong sense of continuity throughout his work.

Do you notice any recent trends in poster design?
I wouldn't consider this a "recent trend," but I have been struck by the surge of hand-printed, limited edition poster production taking place across this country representing a wide variety of personal visions. Often developed hand in hand with their independent music scene, these works have combined the expressive independence first realized during San Francisco's rock poster revolution of the 1960s and the do-it-yourself approach of the 1980s punk scene. Getting their hands dirty and engaging in the entire process has led many designers to challenge themselves to produce the most creative solution not only in terms of design but also on press. The inevitable hits and misses often lead to success after success.

How do posters stand out from other art forms?
A poster's impact is immediate. Again, the purpose of any poster is to attract the eye in the briefest of intervals. It can be the perfect melding of design and marketing. It has a message… sometimes.

Darrin Alfred joined the Denver Art Museum in 2007 and is the AIGA Associate Curator of Graphic Design. Alfred is curator of The Psychedelic Experience: Rock Posters from the San Francisco Bay Area, 1965-1971 (2009), an exhibition organized by the Denver Art Museum. Previously, he served as Assistant Curator in the Department of Architecture and Design at the San Francisco Museum of Modern Art (SFMOMA). The recipient of a Master's degree in Landscape Architecture from the University of Colorado in 1998, Alfred has curated several architecture and design exhibitions including Fantasy and Function: The Furniture of John Dickinson, STREET CRED San Francisco: Architecture and the Pedestrian Experience, and Belles Lettres: The Art of Typography, among many others. Alfred has recently contributed to the forthcoming catalogue raisonné for the Brazilian furniture designers Humberto and Fernando Campana.

(page 12) Darrin Alfred headshot: Courtesy of the Denver Art Museum, Photographer Jeff Wells; (page 14) Rick Griffin, Flying Eyeball / Jimi Hendrix ExperienRick Griffin, Flying Eyeball / Jimi Hendrix Experience, John Mayall and the Blues Breakers, Fillmore Auditorium/ Winterland, San Francisco, 1968. Denver Art Museum Collection: Partial gift of David and Sheryl Tippit; partial purchase with Architecture, Design, and Graphics Department Acquisition Funds; and Volunteer Endowment Funds in honor of R. Craig Miller. Courtesy of the Denver Art Museum © Bill Graham Archives, LLC. www.Wolfgangsvault.com; (page 15) Dylan Poster, Designer: Milton Glaser

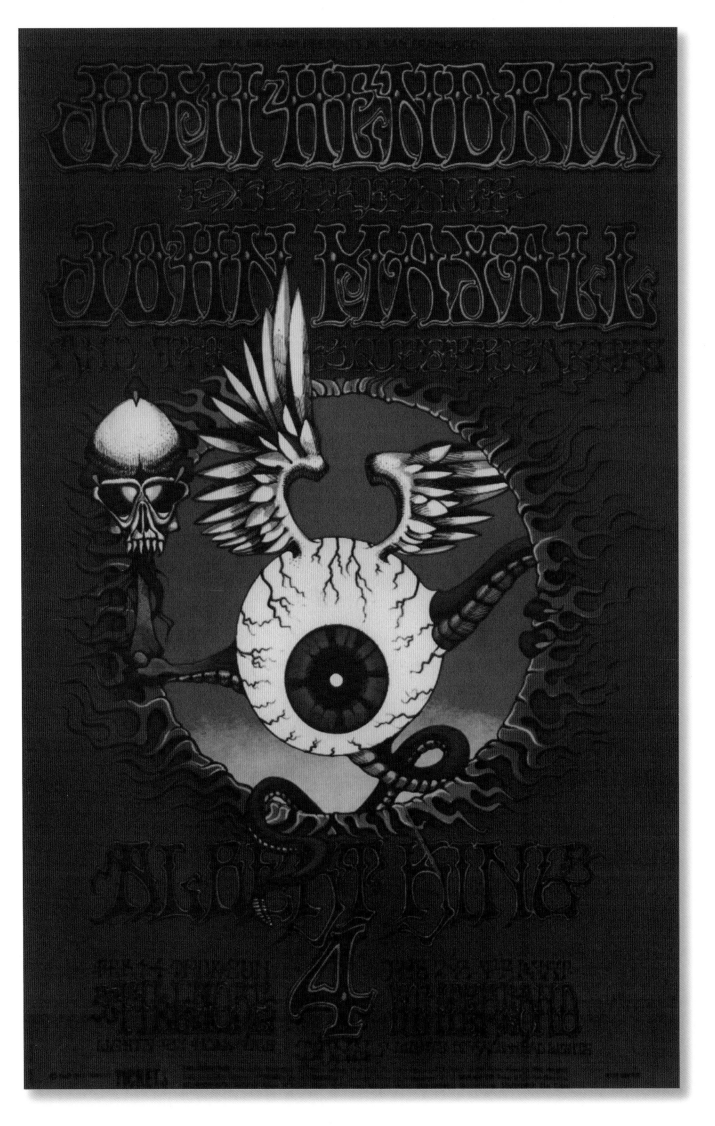

Museums
with Poster
Collections

American Red Cross Museum
1730 E St NW
Washington, DC 20006, USA
Tel (202) 639 3300

Dansk Plakat Museum
Aby Bibliotek
Ludvig Feilbergsvej 7
DK 8230 Åbyhøj, Denmark
Tel + 45 8615 3345

Denver Art Museum
100 W 14th Avenue Pkwy
Denver, CO 80204, USA
Tel (720) 865 5000

The Design Museum
28 Shad Thames
London, SE1, England
Tel +44 20 7403 6933

Ginza Graphic Gallery
Dai Nippon Printing Co., Ltd.*
DNP Ginza Building 1F
7-7-2 Ginza Chuo-ku
Tokyo 104-0061, Japan
Tel 03 3571 5206

Glasgow Gallery of Modern Art
Royal Exchange Square, Glasgow
Lanarkshire G1 3AH, Scotland
Tel 0141 287 3050

Imperial War Museum
Lambeth Road
London SE1 6HZ, England
Tel +44 20 7416 5320

The Lahti Poster Museum*
Vesijärvenkatu 11A, Box 113
Lahti, Finland
Tel +358 3 814 4546

Musee de la Publicite
107, Rue de Rivoli
75001 Paris, France
Tel 331 44 55 57 50

Museum fur Gestaltung Zurich*
Ausstellungsstr. 60, CH-8005
Zurich, Switzerland
Tel +41 43 446 67 67

The Museum of Modern Art*
11 West 53 Street
New York, NY 10019-5497, USA
Tel (212) 708 9400

San Francisco Museum
of Modern Art
151 3rd Street, San Francisco
CA 94103, USA
Tel (415) 357-4000

Smithsonian American
Art Museum
8th & G Sts NW
Washington, DC 20001, USA
Tel (202) 633 1000

State Museum of
Applied Arts, Munich*
Pinakothek der Moderne
Barer Straße 40
80333 Munich, Germany
Tel +49 89 / 2 38 05 360

Victoria and Albert Museum
V&A South Kensington
Cromwell Road
London SW7 2RL, England
Tel: +44 20 7942 2000

Wilanów Poster Museum
10/16 St Kostki Potockiego Street
02-958 Warszawa, Poland
Tel +48 22 842 48 48

* Previously featured in past
Graphis Poster Annuals

This is a basic list of museums that
contain Poster Collections. If you are
a Poster Museums not listed above,
please contact to us through our
website, www.graphis.com.

Opposite page: Frida/Diego poster by Pirtle Design Inc

pg. 37
Category: Competition
Title: Solidarity / Client: National Design Center / Firm: Mark
Gowing Design / Art Director, Creative Director, Designer,
Photographer, Typographer: Mark Gowing

pg. 49
Category: Education
Title: IDEA / Client: ALU Sarajevo / Firm: SVI Design /
Art Director, Creative Director, Designer, Photographer,
Typographer: Mark Gowing

pgs. 104~107
Category: Fashion
Title: Pleats Please Sushi / Client: Issey Miyake Inc. /
Firm: Taku Satoh Design Office, Inc. / Art Director:
Taku Satoh / Designers: Taku Satoh, Teppei Yuyama /
Photographer: Yasuaki Yoshinagag

pgs. 111~112
Category: Festivals
Title: Sing for Gough / Client: Gough Street Festicval /
Firm: Eric Chan Design Co. Ltd. / Art Directors, Designers:
Eric Chan, Iris Yu / Creative Director, Design Director:
Eric Chan / Photographer: Tim Lau

pg. 150
Category: Music
Title: latespot / Client: jazz festival willisau / Firm:
gggrafik-design / Art Director, Artist, Creative Director,
Designer, Typographer: Goetz Gramlich / Print Producer,
Printer: Gerscher Siebdruck / Production: Company gggrafik

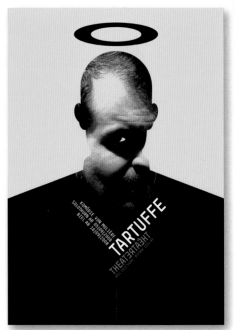

pg. 221
Category: Theater
Title: Tartuffe / Client: Theater Biel Solothurn /
Firm: Atelier Bundi / Account Director, Agency Producer,
Art Director, Artist, Creative Director, Design Director,
Designer, Photographer, Typography: Stephan Bundi /
Printer: Serigraphie Uldry / Production Company:
Theater Biel Solothurm / Project Manager: Birgit Achatz

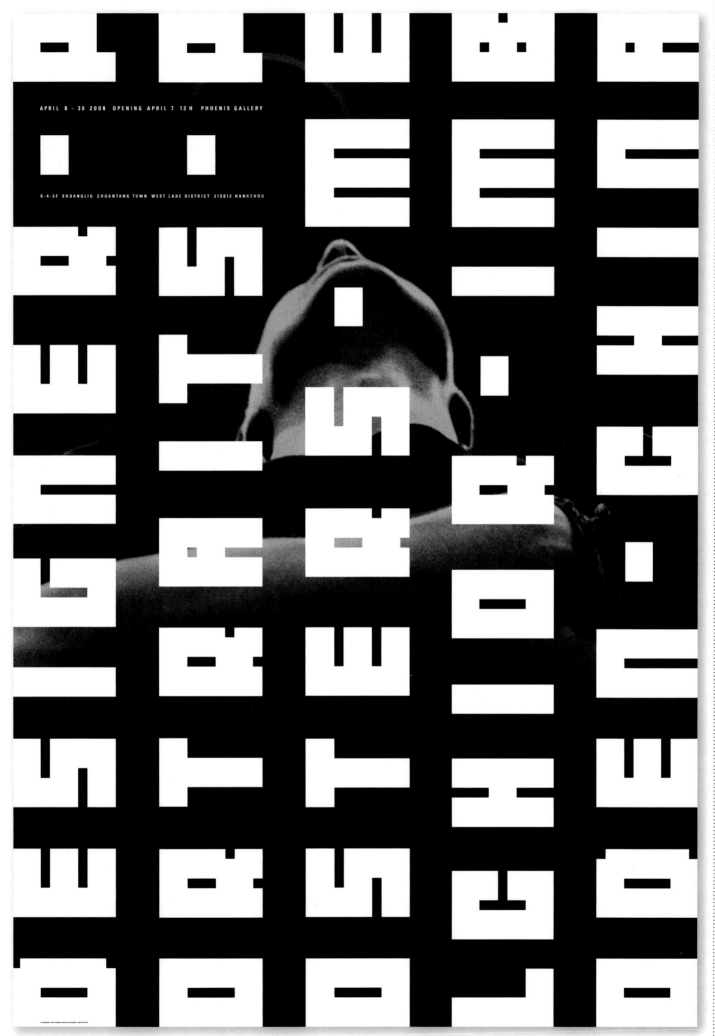

APRIL 8 – 30 2008 OPENING APRIL 7 12 H   PHOENIX GALLERY

8-4-3F SHUANGLIU ZHUANTANG TOWN WEST LAKE DISTRICT 310012 HANGZHOU

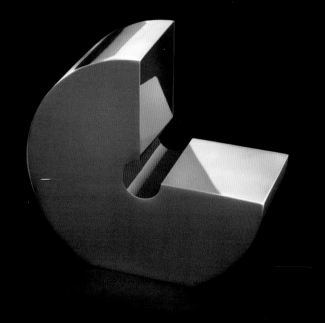

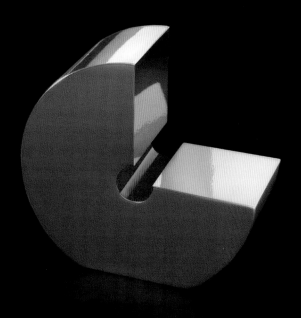

Graphis Platinum & Gold Award Winners by Location

The Americas		
North America:	Estonia 000	Equatorial Guinea 000
Canada 005	Latvia 000	Rwanda 000
United States 102	Lithuania 000	**Southern Africa**
American Island Areas:	**Western Europe**	Angola 000
American Samoa 000	Austria 000	Malawi 000
Guam 000	Belgium 000	Mozambique 000
Mexico 000	France 000	Namibia 000
Northern Marianis 000	Germany 019	South Africa 000
Palau 000	Ireland 000	Swaziland 000
Puerto Rico 000	Italy 000	Zambia 000
Virgin Islands 000	Netherlands 006	Zimbabwe 000
Caribbean:	Portugal 002	**East Africa**
Antigua and Barbuda 000	Spain 004	Eritrea 000
Bahamas 000	Switzerland 011	Ethiopia 000
Barbados 000	UK 007	Kenya 000
Cayman Island 000	**Commonwealth of**	Somalia 000
Cuba 000	**Independent States**	Sudan 000
Dominica 000	Armenia 000	Tanzania 000
Dominican Republic 000	Azerbaijan 000	Uganda 000
Grenada 000	Belarus 000	**West Africa**
Haiti 000	Georgia 000	Burkina Faso 000
Jamaica 000	Kazakstan 000	Cote D'ivoire 000
St. Kitts and Nevis 000	Kyrgyzstan 000	Ghana 000
St. Lucia 000	Moldova 000	Guinea 000
St. Vincent&The Grenadines 000	Russian Federation 001	Guinea-Bissau 000
Trinidad&Tobago 000	Tajikistan 000	Liberia 000
Central America:	Turkmenistan 000	Mauritania 000
Belize 000	Ukraine 000	Niger 000
Costa Rica 000	Uzbekistan 000	Nigeria 000
El Salvador 000	**Southeast Europe**	Senegal 000
Guatemala 000	Albania 000	Sierra Leone 000
Honduras 000	Bosnia-Herzegovina 000	Togo 000
Nicaragua 000	Bulgaria 000	**Asia&Oceania**
Panama 000	Croatia 001	**Asia:**
South America:	Cyprus 000	**East Asia**
Argentina 000	Greece 000	China 004
Bolivia 000	Macedonia 000	Japan 019
Brazil 000	Malta 000	Mongolia 000
Chile 000	Serbia&Montenegro 000	North Korea 000
Colombia 000	Slovenia 000	South Korea 002
Ecuador 000	Turkey 002	Taiwan 001
Guyana 000	**Middle East:**	**Southwest Asia**
Paraguay 000	Bahrain 000	Brunei Darussalam 000
Peru 000	Iran 000	Cambodia 000
Uruguay 000	Iraq 000	Indonesia 000
Venezuela 000	Israel / Occupied Territories 002	Laos 000
Europe&Africa	Jordan 000	Malaysia 000
Europe:	Kuwait 000	Myanmar 000
Northern Europe	Lebanon 000	Philippines 000
Aland 000	Palestinian Authority 000	Singapore 000
Denmark 001	Saudi Arabia 000	Thailand 000
Faroe Islands 000	Syria 000	Timor-Leste 000
Finland 003	UAE 000	Viet Nam 000
Greenland 000	Yemen 000	**South Asia**
Iceland 000	**Africa:**	Afghanistan 000
Karelia 000	**North Africa**	Bangladesh 000
Kola Peninsula 000	Algeria 000	Bhutan 000
Norway 003	Egypt 000	India 000
Sweden 001	Libya 000	Maldives 000
Svalbard 000	Morocco West Sahara 000	Nepal 000
Eathern Europe	Tunisia 000	Pakistan 000
Czech Republic 000	**Central Africa**	Sri Lanka 000
Hungary 000	Burundi 000	**Oceania:**
Poland 000	Cameroon 000	Australia 007
Romania 000	Cent. African Rep. 000	Fiji 000
Slovak Republic 000	Chad 000	New Zealand 000
Baltic States	Congo 000	Papua New Guinea 000
	DR Congo 000	Solomon Islands 000

Total Winning Entries **197**

EVENTS FALL 2008   COLUMBIA UNIVERSITY   GSAPP   WWW.ARCH.COLUMBIA.EDU/EVENTS

EVENTS FALL 2008   COLUMBIA UNIVERSITY   GSAPP   WWW.ARCH.COLUMBIA.EDU/EVENTS

Sagmeister, Inc. | Columbia Graduate School of Architecture, Planning and Preservation | Architecture**23**

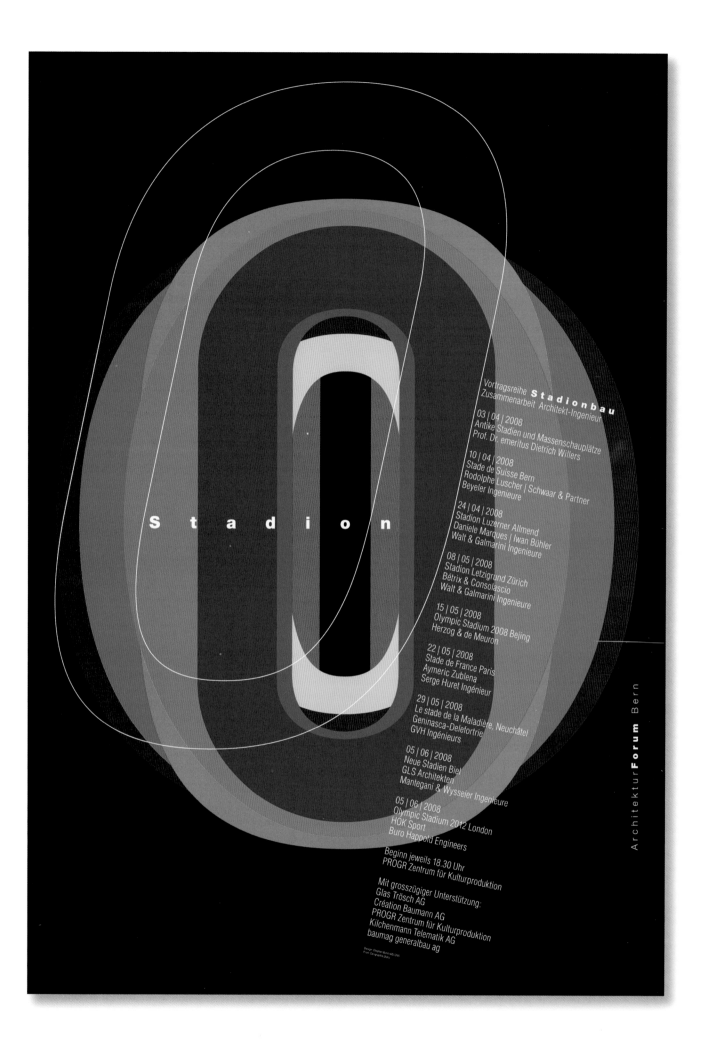

Vortragsreihe **Stadionbau**
Zusammenarbeit Architekt-Ingenieur

03 | 04 | 2008
Antike Stadien und Massenschauplätze
Prof. Dr. emeritus Dietrich Willers

10 | 04 | 2008
Stade de Suisse Bern
Rodolphe Luscher | Schwaar & Partner
Beyeler Ingenieure

24 | 04 | 2008
Stadion Luzerner Allmend
Daniele Marques | Iwan Bühler
Walt & Galmarini Ingenieure

08 | 05 | 2008
Stadion Letzigrund Zürich
Bétrix & Consolascio
Walt & Galmarini Ingenieure

15 | 05 | 2008
Olympic Stadium 2008 Bejing
Herzog & de Meuron

22 | 05 | 2008
Stade de France Paris
Aymeric Zublena
Serge Huret Ingénieur

29 | 05 | 2008
Le stade de la Maladière, Neuchâtel
Geninasca-Delefortrie
GVH Ingénieurs

05 | 06 | 2008
Neue Stadien Biel
GLS Architekten
Mantegani & Wysseier Ingenieure

05 | 06 | 2008
Olympic Stadium 2012 London
HOK Sport
Buro Happold Engineers

Beginn jeweils 18.30 Uhr
PROGR Zentrum für Kulturproduktion

Mit grosszügiger Unterstützung:
Glas Trösch AG
Création Baumann AG
PROGR Zentrum für Kulturproduktion
Kilchenmann Telematik AG
baumag generalbau ag

Stadion

ArchitekturForum Bern

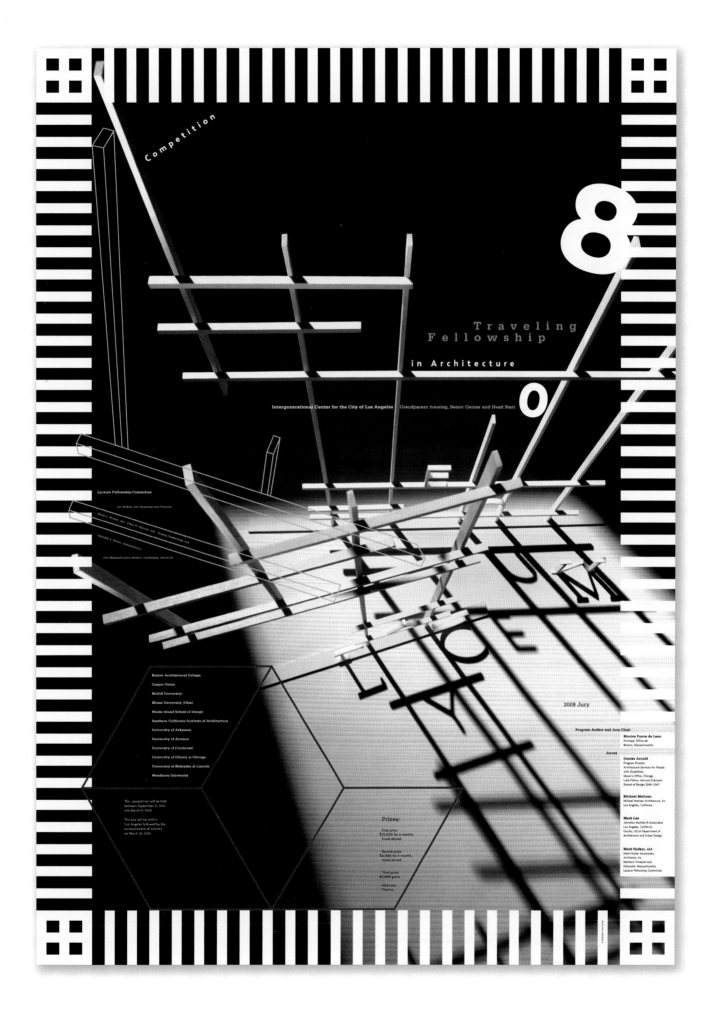

Competition

8

Traveling
Fellowship

in Architecture

0

Intergenerational Center for the City of Los Angeles   Grandparent housing, Senior Center and Head Start

Lyceum Fellowship Committee

Jan McKee, AIA Chairman and Traveler

Mark A. Hutker, AIA   Peter N Vincent, AIA   Joseph Krakoroanski, AIA

Jennifer A. Swain, Administrator

1000 Massachusetts Avenue Cambridge, MA 02138

Boston Architectural College

Cooper Union

McGill University

Miami University (Ohio)

Rhode Island School of Design

Southern California Institute of Architecture

University of Arkansas

University of Arizona

University of Cincinnati

University of Illinois at Chicago

University of Nebraska at Lincoln

Woodbury University

The competition will be held
between September 15, 2007
and March 19, 2008.

The jury will be held in
Los Angeles followed by the
announcement of winners
on March 28, 2008

Prizes:

First prize:
$10,000 for 6 months
travel abroad

Second prize:
$6,000 for 3 months
travel abroad

Third prize:
$1,000 grant

Alternate:
Citation

2008 Jury

Program Author and Jury Chair

Monica Ponce de Leon
Principal, Office dA
Boston, Massachusetts

Jurors

Denise Arnold
Program Director
Architectural Services for People
with Disabilities
Mayor's Office, Chicago
Loeb Fellow, Harvard Graduate
School of Design 2006-2007

Michael Maltzan
Michael Maltzan Architecture, Inc
Los Angeles, California

Mark Lee
Johnston Marklee & Associates
Los Angeles, California
Faculty, UCLA Department of
Architecture and Urban Design

Mark Hutker, AIA
Mark Hutker Associates,
Architects, Inc.
Martha's Vineyard and
Falmouth, Massachusetts
Lyceum Fellowship Committee

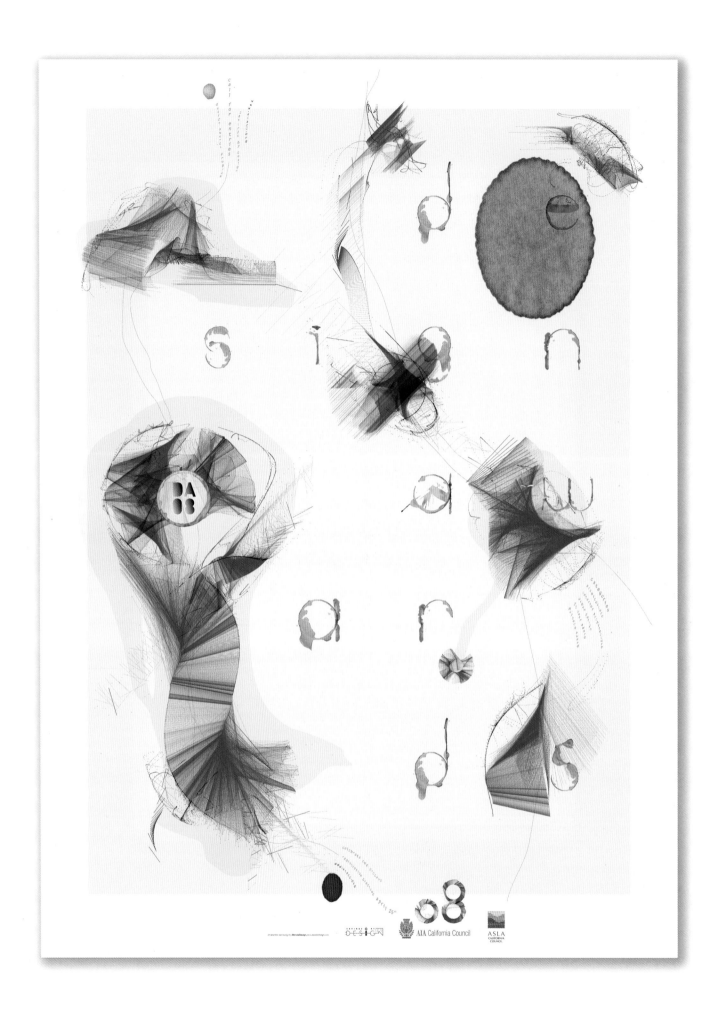

CINANIMA

32º FESTIVAL INTERNACIONAL DE CINEMA DE ANIMAÇÃO · 32nd INTERNATIONAL ANIMATED FILM FESTIVAL
ORGANIZAÇÃO: NASCENTE-COOPERATIVA DE ACÇÃO CULTURAL, CRL./CÂMARA MUNICIPAL DE ESPINHO

Design:JOÃO MACHADO

10.16.NOV.
2008

ESPINHO
PORTUGAL

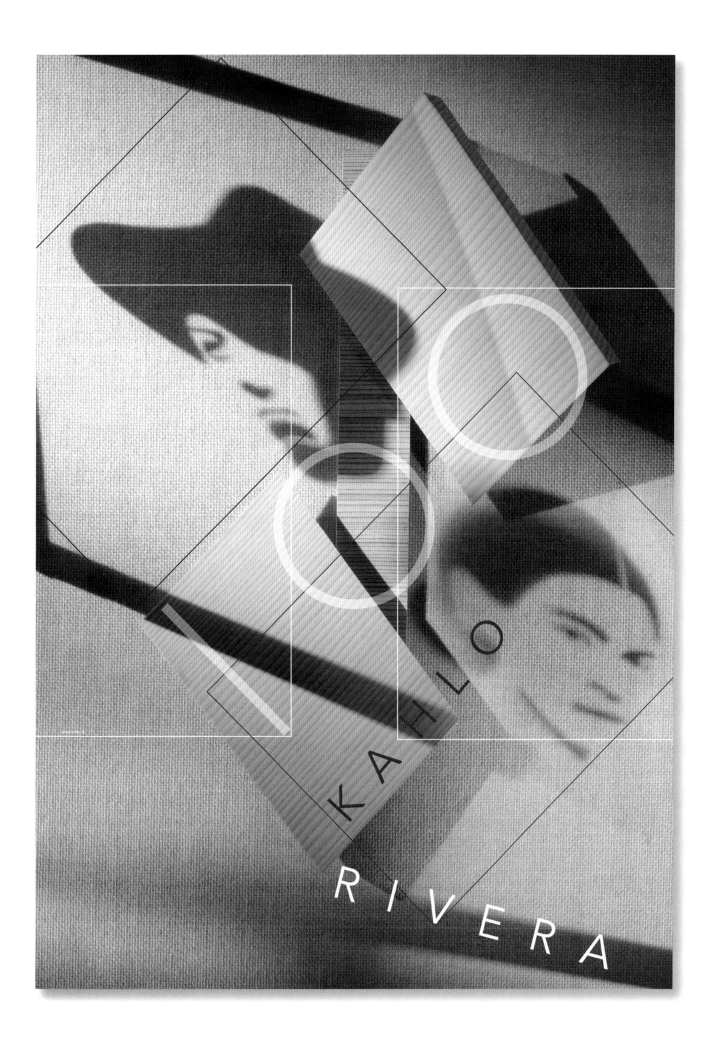

KAHLO

RIVERA

remembering

2008

FRIDA AND DIEGO

MALCOLM GREAR

29 JUNE 2008

icsid
IDA

International Council
of Societies of Industrial Design
A Partner of the International
Design Alliance

RLD INDUSTRIAL DESIGN DAY

NIKKEI BP ADVERTISING AWARDS 2008

送り出したすべての力を、讃えたい。

Design by Shin Matsunaga

第22回コイズミ国際学生照明デザインコンペ

ENTRIES INVITED

Theme
In search of the Way of Light...
Earth-friendly Lighting

Light can give life to inanimate objects. In this sense, we can say that it is life itself.
Meanwhile, using energy efficiently and caring for the environment are both unavoidable challenges for all people living in the 21st century.
We would like you to design lighting with which people can work for the earth together, despite the differences in their economic backgrounds.
Do not focus too much on the design theme and try to create a new form of lighting.

● Awards (Tax included) : Gold Award (1) = Certificate of award and ¥1,000,000 / Silver Award (2) = Certificate of award and ¥300,000 / Bronze Award (5) = Certificate of award and ¥100,000 /
Honorable Mention (Limited Number) = Certificate of award and prize

● Head Juror : Kenji Ekuan (Industrial Designer : Japan)
● Jury Panels : Kiyonori Kikutake (Architect : Japan) / Shoei Yoh (Architect, Designer : Japan) / Angelo Cortesi (Industrial Designer : Italy) / Patrick Whitney (Designer : U.S.A.) /
The representatives from Koizumi Lighting Technology Corporation

● Entry Eligibility : Any student from institute of learning as of September 1, 2008 ● Application Period : September 1, 2008 to January 31, 2009
● Preliminary Competition Judging Period : March 2009 ● Notification of Preliminary Competition Winners : April 2009 ● Final Competition : May 2009

● Sponsor : Koizumi Lighting Technology Corporation
● Affiliated Associations : Japan Industrial Design Promotion Organization / Japan Industrial Designers Association / International Council of Societies of Industrial Design

● Design Competition on the Web : Designs that have passed the first-round of jury will be put up on our web page, where we will have the Design Competition on the Web with the votes from
selected Teachers, Architects, Designers, Journalists and all others from around the world.
Best Design Award (1) = Certificate and prize / Excellent Design Award (2) = Certificate and prize

● Where to Enter
Japan — Mr.Yoshino : Office of Koizumi International Lighting Design Competition for Students
Koizumi Lighting Technology Corporation 3-3-7 Bingomachi, Chuo-ku, Osaka, 541-0051 JAPAN
TEL : +81-(0)6-6262-1369 / FAX : +81-(0)6-6266-7845 / compe@koizumi.co.jp

U.S.A. — Ms.Sophie Ugumori : Koizumi Lighting Design
5 Eason Drive Ridge, NY 11961, USA
TEL / FAX : +1-631-345-3610 / koizumi@usa.com

Italy — Ms.Kazumi Kurihara : Koizumi Compe
Viale Monza 325, 20126 Milano, ITALY
TEL : +39-02-2570380 / koizumicompe@tiscali.it

China · Dongguan — Mr.Hu Xiao : Koizumi Electric Home Appliances Technology Consulting Co., Ltd.
3F, No28, Wenquannan Lu, Shilong Town, Dongguan city, Guandong Provinces 523325, CHINA
TEL : +86-(0)769-86189576 / FAX : +86-(0)769-86189579 / hx@koizumi-hk.com

China · Shanghai — Ms.Setty Chou : Koizumi Lighting Technology(Shanghai) Co., Ltd.
Rm.1201, Tianyi Mansion No.251 Xiao Mu Qiao Road, Shanghai, CHINA
TEL : +86-(0)21-34160126 / FAX : +86-(0)21-54960450 / sety@koizumi.com.cn

Korea — Ms.Soo-hyun Lee : Hwangduck Engineering Co., Ltd.
1F 106, Hyundai Hyperion Business Center, #805, Hannam1-dong, Yongsan-gu, Seoul 140-210, KOREA
TEL : +82-(0)2-794-0801 / FAX : +82-(0)2-798-0860 / mail@hwangduck.com

Design by Shin Matsunaga

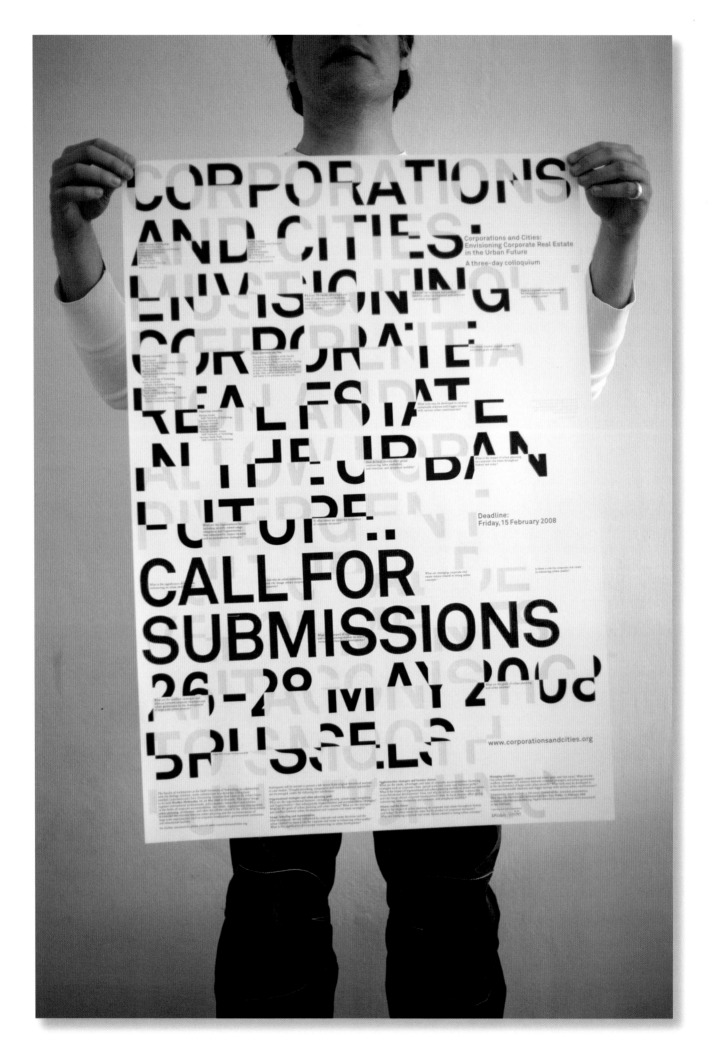

OBJECT DESIGNERS
FUNCTIONAL. EXPERIMENTAL.
CONCEPTUAL. MANUFACTURED.
HANDCRAFTED. FURNITURE.
APPLIANCES. ACCESSORIES.
OBJECTS. IDEAS. INNOVATIONS.
ARE YOU THE NEXT BIG THING?
REGISTER BY JULY 31 AT
WWW.SOYA.COM.AU

**THINK BIG.
STAND OUT.
WIN THE WORLD.**
THE QANTAS SPIRIT OF YOUTH AWARDS
(SOYA) OFFERS INDUSTRIAL AND OBJECT
DESIGNERS AGED 30 AND UNDER
THE CHANCE TO WIN $10,000 IN CASH
AND FLIGHTS AND A PROFESSIONAL
MENTORSHIP WITH ICONIC AUSTRALIAN
DESIGNER MARC NEWSON, WORKING
IN HIS PARIS STUDIO.

QANTAS SPIRIT OF
YOUTH AWARDS 2008

'AROMA' BY SOYA05 WINNER DAVID MANSUETO / DESIGN WWW.FROSTDESIGN.COM.AU

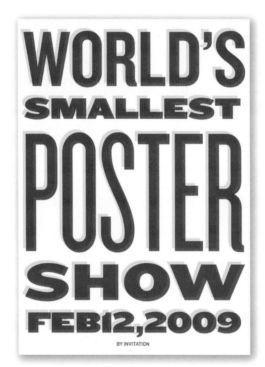

(Actual Size)

TEXAS INSTRUMENTS FOUNDATION PRESENTS

THE NUTCRACKER

FEATURING WENDY WHELAN AND PHILIP NEAL OF NEW YORK CITY BALLET, AND CHRIS JAROSZ FROM "SO YOU THINK YOU CAN DANCE"

NOVEMBER 28-30 AT THE EISEMANN CENTER

TICKETS AVAILABLE AT WWW.EISEMANNCENTER.COM OR BY CALLING THE TICKET OFFICE AT 972.744.4650

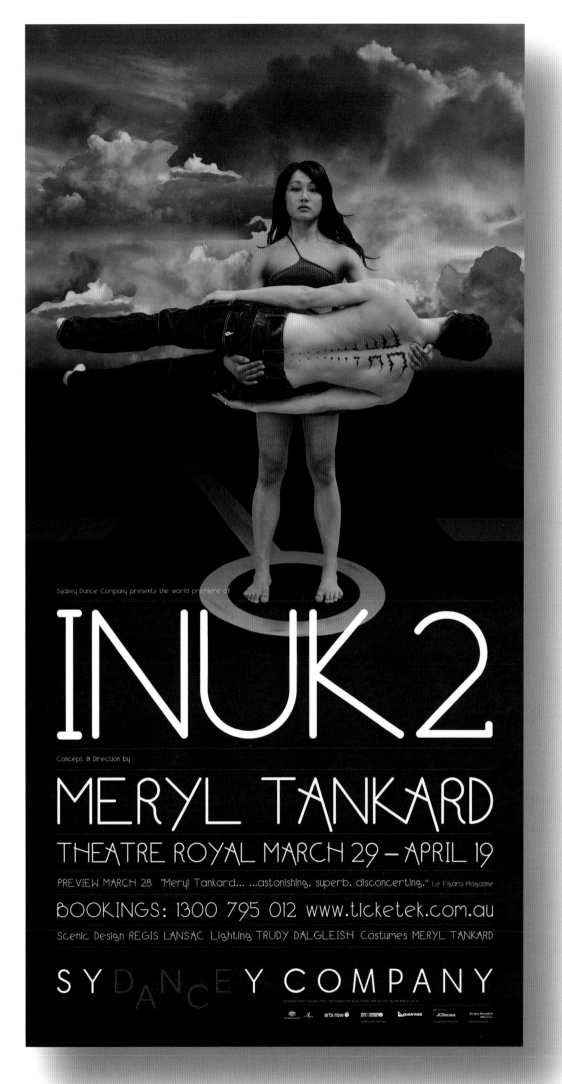

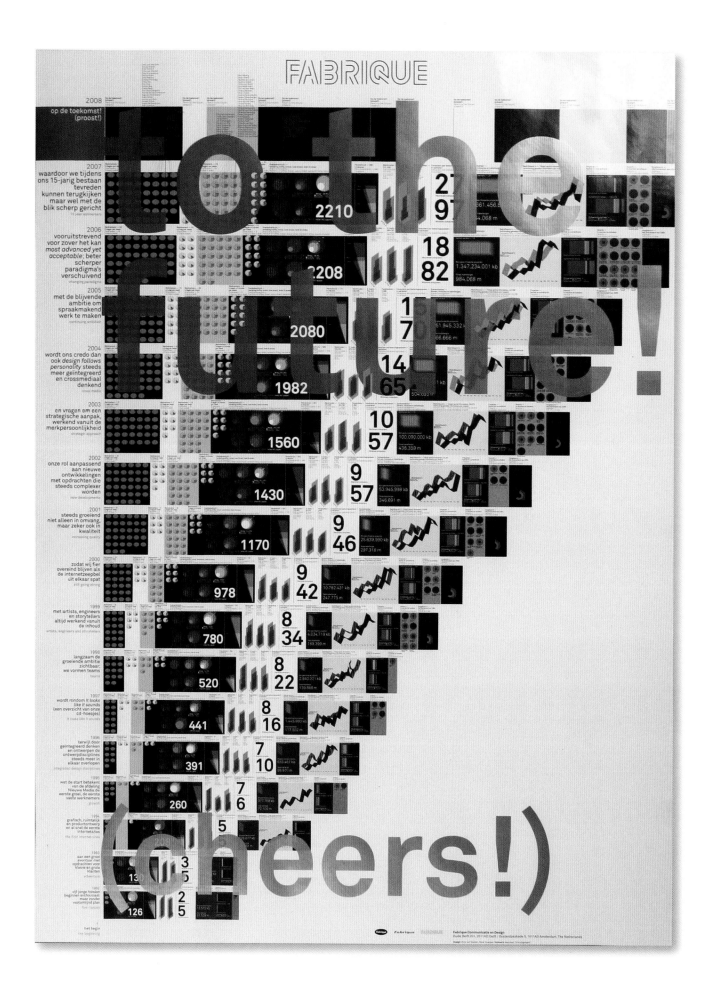

Woody Pirtle
ANTHROPOLOGY
SERIES 1 CIRCA 2008

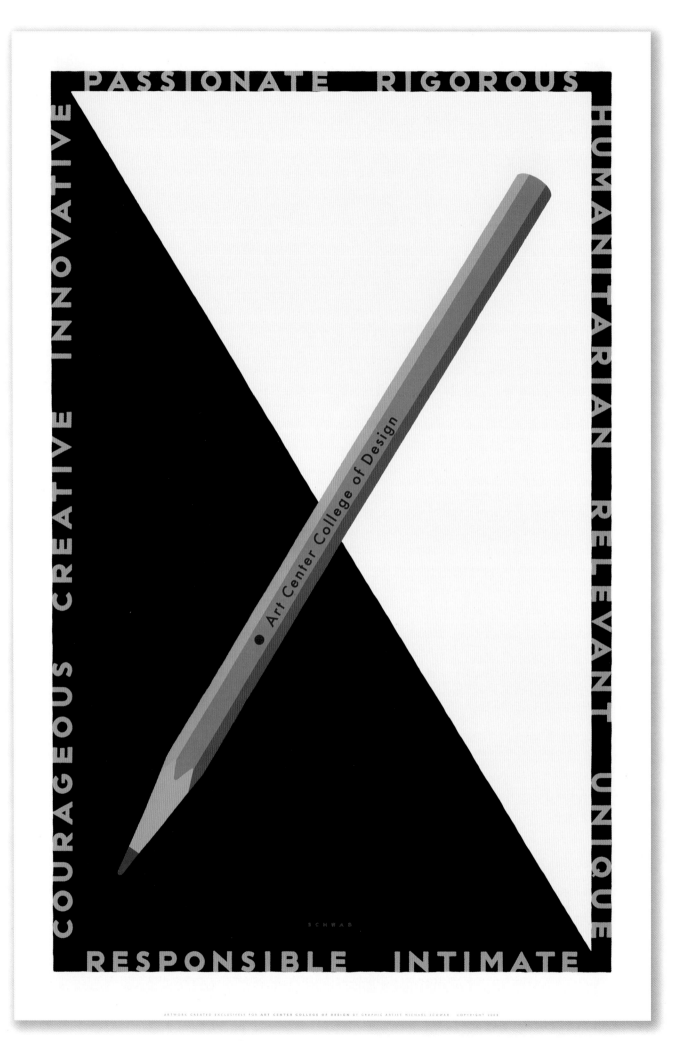

IDEA

The Balancing Act
Michael Braley
VSA Partners, Inc. | New York
Portfolio Center
July 24, 2008 | 10:00 a.m.
Atlanta, Georgia

Portfolio Center welcomes Michael Braley for his design lecture, "The Balancing Act," Thursday, July 24, at 10:00 a.m. Michael Braley is the Design Director at VSA Partners, Inc., New York. His work has been recognized internationally and is in the permanent collections of the San Francisco Museum of Modern Art, the Chicago Athenaeum Museum of Architecture and Design and the Museum für Kunst und Gewerbe in Hamburg, Germany. His clients have included American Express, AIGA, The Black Book, Ellen Vodka, The Fine Arts Museum of San Francisco, IBM, Strichaw and Tanqueray. His work has appeared in numerous publications and exhibitions including: British Design and Art Direction, The Cho Awards, I.D., Graftik (UK), Graphis, Type Directors Club, Communication Arts, American Center for Design 100 Show, The AR100 Show, The Art Directors Club of New York, The One Show, AIGA 365, URSIc Step 100, and Print. Previous to joining VSA Partners, Braley was a member of Cahan & Associates, San Francisco, for nine years. Braley has taught typography at the California College of the Arts (CCA) and has lectured and led workshops at universities and professional organizations around the nation.

The Balancing Act
Michael Braley
VSA Partners, Inc. | New York
Portfolio Center
July 24, 2008 | 10:00 a.m.
Atlanta, Georgia

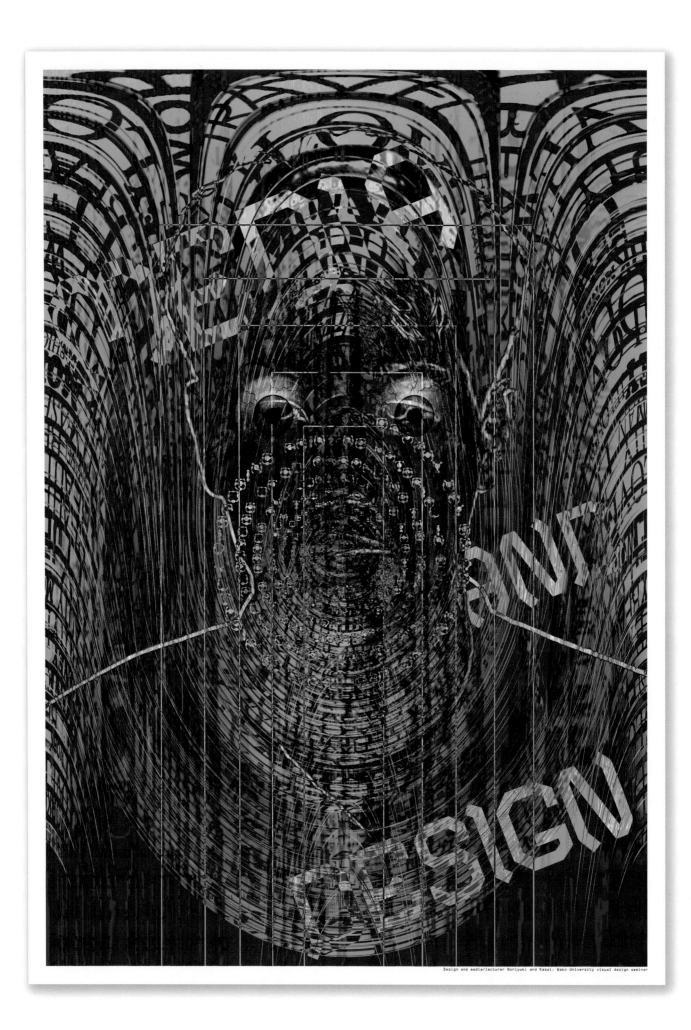

Design and media/lecturer Noriyuki and Kasai- Wako University visual design seminar

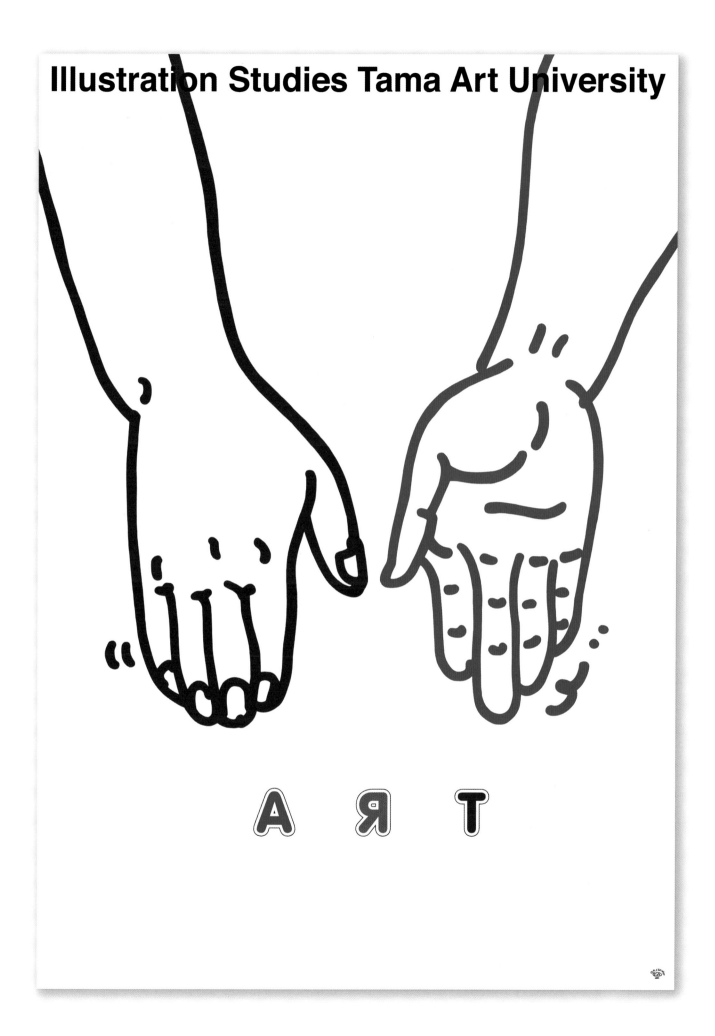

NO T'EQUIVOQUIS. CADA COSA AL SEU LLOC

SEPARANT LES DEIXALLES, A RODA MILLOREM EL RECICLATGE

AJUNTAMENT DE RODA DE TER
Regidoria de serveis
Regidoria de medi ambient

RodaSostenible

Punt
d'Atenció
Ambiental
Telèfon
93 850 00 75

Agència de
Residus de
Catalunya

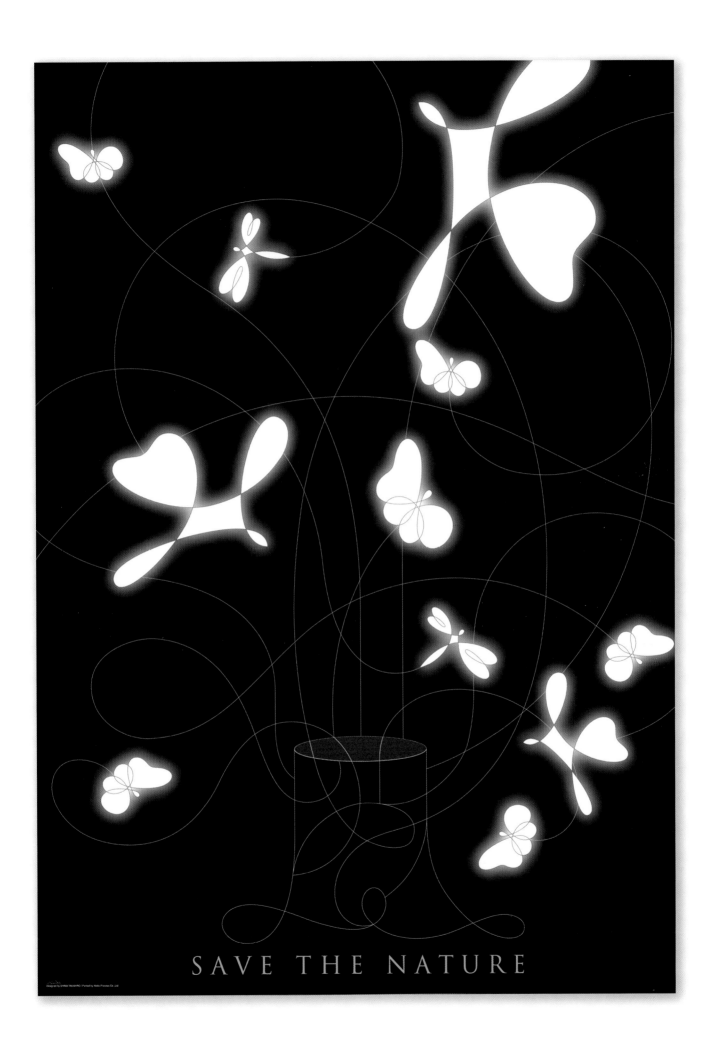

SAVE THE NATURE

1 week's garbage. 1 person

52 weeks in the year. 20 million people in Australia. 6.6 billion people in the world

The above is a visual record of the rubbish that I threw out over the week of 12–19th June 2008. A pretty average week.

Australian Poster Annual 2008

FRISKT VATTEN

27
Co
1.70

86
Rn
2.06

MOTHERS FOR NATURAL LAWS | As much as one fourth of all American agricultural lands raise genetically modified (GM) crops with little or no government oversight. Yet in most other countries, the same approach is subject to moratoriums, partially banned, or restricted with stiff legal penalties for non-compliance. Genetically modified foods contain substances that have never been a part of the human food supply. Keep Our Food as Mother Nature Intended. | www.safe-food.org

STEFAN SAGMEISTER
THINGS I HAVE LEARNED IN MY LIFE SO FAR

MUMOK HOFSTALLUNGEN, MUSEUMSPLATZ 1, 1070 WIEN
FREITAG, 4. JULI 2008 BEGINN: **19:00 UHR** EINTRITT: **10€**

DESIGN AUSTRIA MITGLIEDER SOWIE RAIFFEISEN CLUB-MITGLIEDER KOSTENLOS
ANMELDUNG ERFORDERLICH UNTER SAGMEISTER@DESIGNFORUM.AT
RAIFFEISEN VERLOST 5 SIGNIERTE STEFAN SAGMEISTER BÜCHER „THINGS I HAVE LEARNED IN MY LIFE SO FAR"
IN KOOPERATION MIT DER RAIFFEISENBANK IN WIEN

photo:
HENRY LEUTWYLER

AN EXPERIMENT IN COLLABORATION

BRIEF:
A catalogue to accompany an exhibition about the process of collaborative art.

SOLUTION:
Each visitor gets a huge printed poster and some simple instructions for cutting, folding and binding.

The audience performs the final act of collaboration by producing the exhibiton catalogue themselves.

RESULT:
1000 posters, 1000 unique catalogues.

THE ART:

MICHAEL PYBUS, **ARTIST** +
DAZED & CONFUSED **MAGAZINE**

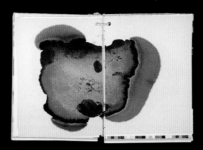

JACKSON WEBB, **ARTISTS COLLABORATORS** +
DORA TANG, **BIOPHYSICIST**

KAREN TANG, **SCULPTOR** +
DANIEL SANDERSON, **ARCHITECT**

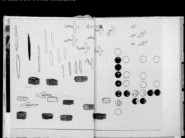

DANIEL BAKER, **ARTIST/ANIMATOR** +
RICKY HAGGETT, **COMPUTER GAME DESIGNER**

MICHAEL PYBUS, **ARTIST** +
DAZED & CONFUSED **MAGAZINE**

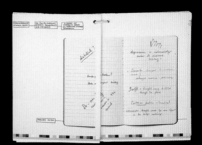

GEMMA ANDERSON, **PRINTMAKER** +
DOCTOR TIM McINERNY, **FORENSIC PSYCHIATRIST**

DANIEL BAKER, **ARTIST/ANIMATOR** +
RICKY HAGGETT, **COMPUTER GAME DESIGNER**

GEMMA ANDERSON, **PRINTMAKER** +
DR TIM McINERNY, **FORENSIC PSYCHIATRIST**

MICHAEL PYBUS, **ARTIST** +
DAZED & CONFUSED **MAGAZINE**

The Art Directors Club
FESTIVAL of FAME

ALEX BOGUSKY
SIR JOHN HEGARTY
RAY EAMES
R ROGER REMINGTON
M AIRA KALMAN
JOHN MAEDA
BRUCE WEBER

Benefit Gala

JOHN HOCKENBERRY
MASTER of CEREMONIES

november 6 2008

a gathering to celebrate adam eeuwens' 40ᵗʰ birthday.

10.19.2007 8:00 pm
at the neutra: 11009.5 strathmore drive, los angeles, california 90024
rsvp: rebeca@rebecamendez.com

His generation composed the greatest stories of our time. Let's help make his next chapter just as memorable.

For a glimpse into his life, visit grace.inventivhealth.com.

Donate to Grace today.

EXHIBITOR SHOW 09

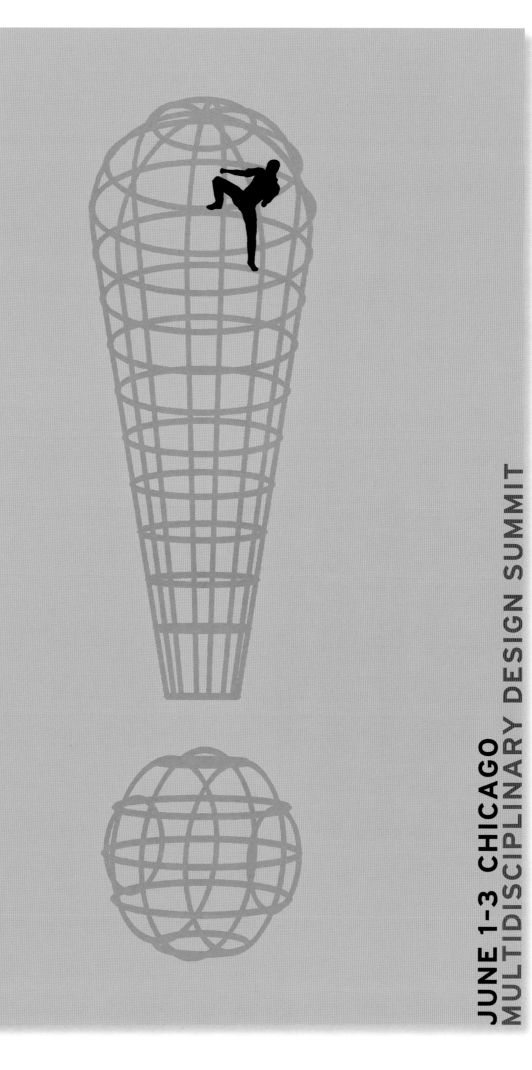

GRAVITY FREE 2009
PLAYGROUND OF FEARLESS THINKERS

JUNE 1–3 CHICAGO
MULTIDISCIPLINARY DESIGN SUMMIT

3ª

SETMANA DE LA GENT GRAN

AJUNTAMENT DE RODA DE TER

Regidoria de Benestar i Família

CASAL D'AVIS

RODA DE TER DE L'1 AL 9 DE JUNY DE 2007

ORGANITZADA PER L'AJUNTAMENT DE RODA DE TER AMB LA COL·LABORACIÓ DE "EL CASAL" D'AVIS

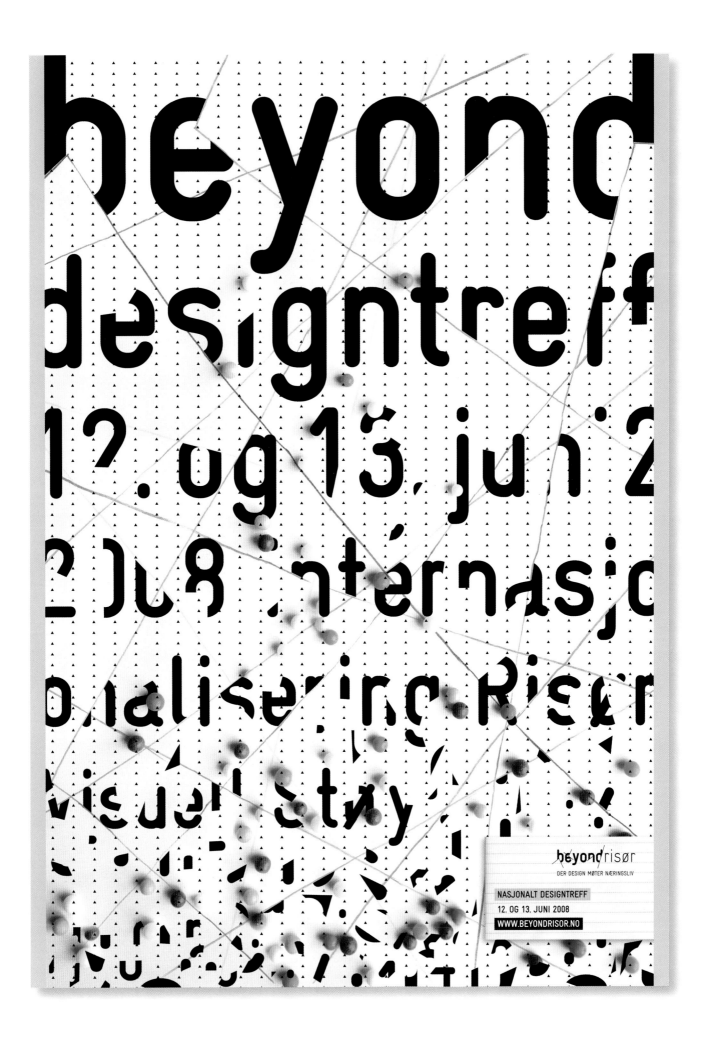

Keith Morris talks type over lunch   Date: Wednesday, 13 February 2008 Time:12:30 /2:00 Location: Berry Bay

JAMES HACKETT BROADCASTING SOON
FRIDAY 03.04.08 1PM | LEVEL 11, 15 BLUE ST

ESPAÑA
PAÍS INVITADO DE HONOR 2009
SPAIN, GUEST COUNTRY OF HONOUR 2009
西班牙: 2009年主宾国

Sueña, piensa, lee… España
Dream Spain, Think Spain, Read Spain
梦想西班牙、思考西班牙、解读西班牙

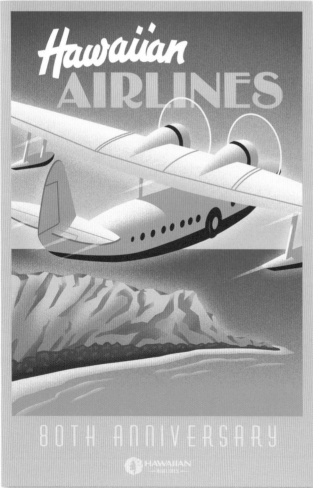

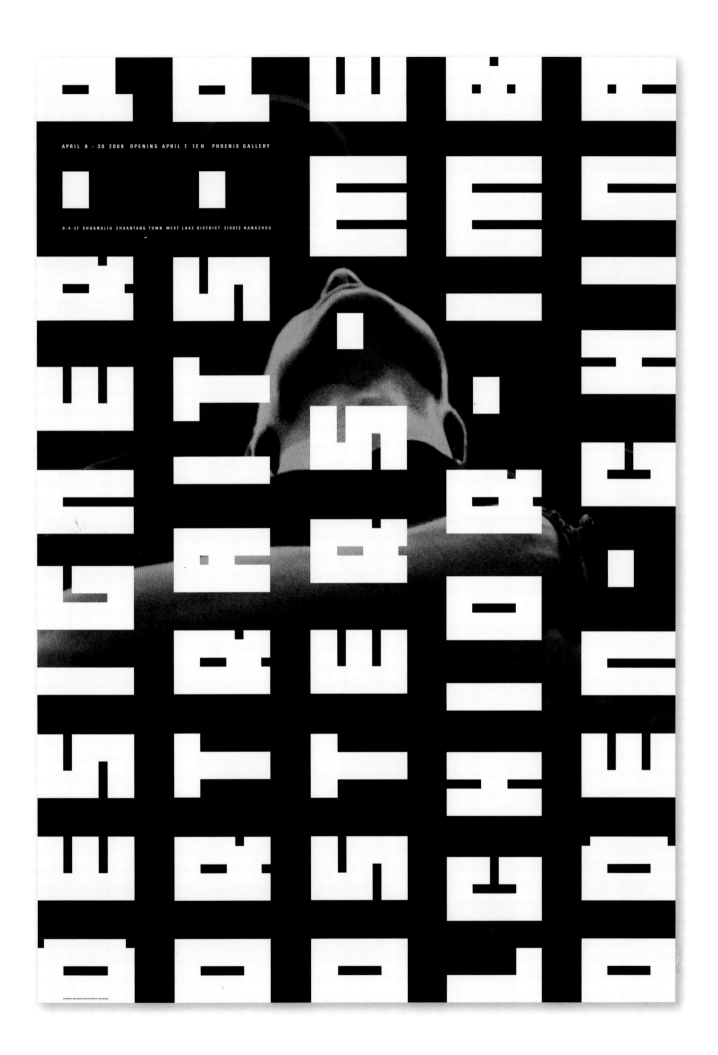

APRIL 8 – 30 2008 OPENING APRIL 7 12 H PHOENIX GALLERY

B-4-3F SHUANGLIU ZHUANTANG TOWN WEST LAKE DISTRICT 310012 HANGZHOU

the double space

erik a

frandsen

10oktober2008–4januar2009

ARoS

det dobbelte rum

Vilh. Kiers Fond, Kulturministeriet, Augustinus Fonden, C.A.C. Fonden, Bikubenfonden/BG Fonden, Politiken–Fonden, Montana, Sparbank, Bendixen Neon

THREE, 2008
DOWNLOADED
NOVEMBER 12 2008
15:48:59
FROM IP NUMBER 213.80.98.130
FROM COUNTRY SWEDEN
DOWNLOAD #2
SIZE 7521 KILOBYTES
ABSOLUT.COM/
HELMUTLANG

IN AN ABSOLUT WORLD
ALLES GLEICH SCHWER
BY HELMUT LANG

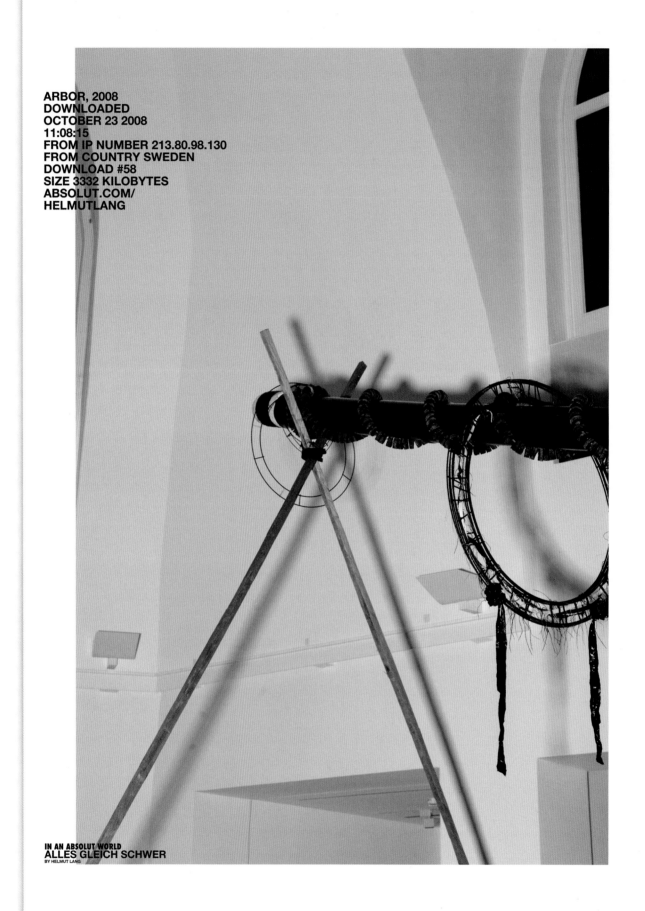

ARBOR, 2008
DOWNLOADED
OCTOBER 23 2008
11:08:15
FROM IP NUMBER 213.80.98.130
FROM COUNTRY SWEDEN
DOWNLOAD #58
SIZE 3332 KILOBYTES
ABSOLUT.COM/
HELMUTLANG

IN AN ABSOLUT WORLD
ALLES GLEICH SCHWER
BY HELMUT LANG

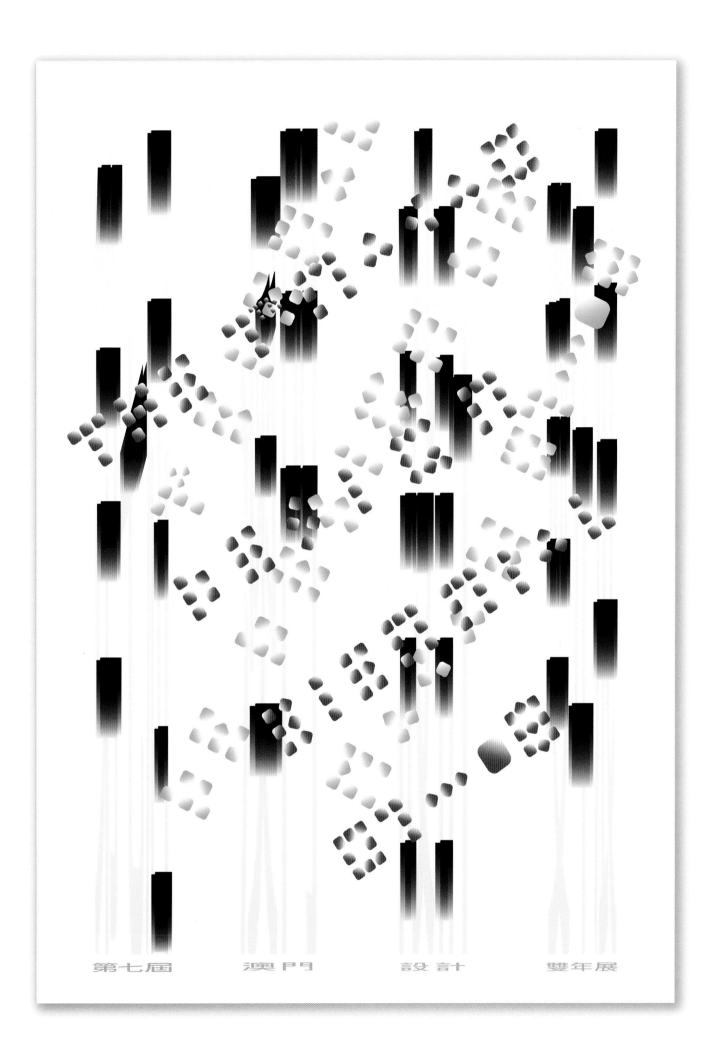

第七屆　　　澳門　　　設計　　　雙年展

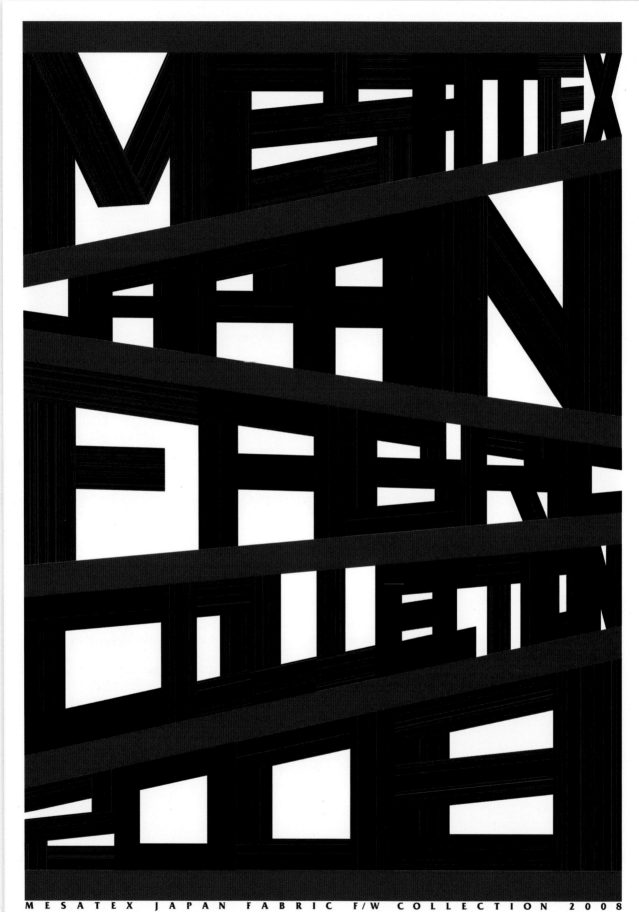

MESATEX JAPAN FABRIC F/W COLLECTION 2008

MESATEX JAPAN Inc. メサテックス・ジャパン株式会社 東京都港区西麻布4-1-11-2F 〒106-0031 2F-4-1-11 NISHIAZABU, MINATO-KU, TOKYO 106-0031 JAPAN TEL 03-3496-1545 FAX 03-5485-2682

A DESIGN INSTALLATION BY ABBOTT MILLER AT PRAZAK PALACE

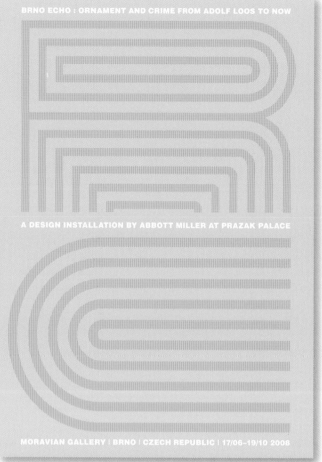

A DESIGN INSTALLATION BY ABBOTT MILLER AT PRAZAK PALACE

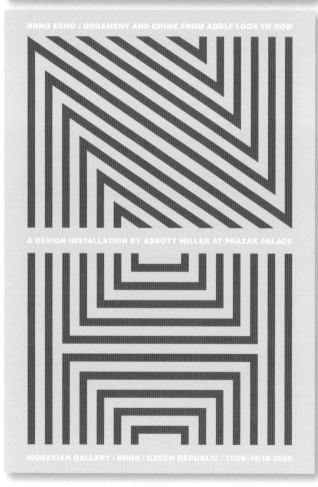

A DESIGN INSTALLATION BY ABBOTT MILLER AT PRAZAK PALACE

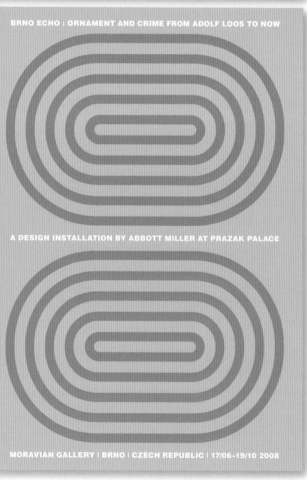

BRNO ECHO : ORNAMENT AND CRIME FROM ADOLF LOOS TO NOW

A DESIGN INSTALLATION BY ABBOTT MILLER AT PRAZAK PALACE

MORAVIAN GALLERY | BRNO | CZECH REPUBLIC | 17/06–19/10 2008

Stolpersteine der Kommunikation
MISSVERSTÄNDNISSE
Ausstellung 6. November 2008 – 17. Mai 2009

MUSEUMSUFERFRANKFURT

Schaumainkai 53, 60596 Frankfurt am Main
Telefon: 069.60 60 0, www.museumsstiftung.de

Dienstag–Freitag 9–18 Uhr
Samstag, Sonntag, Feiertag 11–19 Uhr

Museum für
Kommunikation
Frankfurt

Pentagram Design Ltd., Berlin | Museum of Communication Germany | Exhibitions **94**

WENN ICH
SONNTAGS
IN MEIN'
KINO GEH'

TON – FILM – MUSIK
1929 – 1933

20. 12. 2007 – 27. 4. 2008

Museum für Film und Fernsehen
Potsdamer Straße 2
S-/U-Bahn Potsdamer Platz
www.deutsche-kinemathek.de

Dienstag bis Sonntag 10 – 18 Uhr
Donnerstag 10 – 20 Uhr

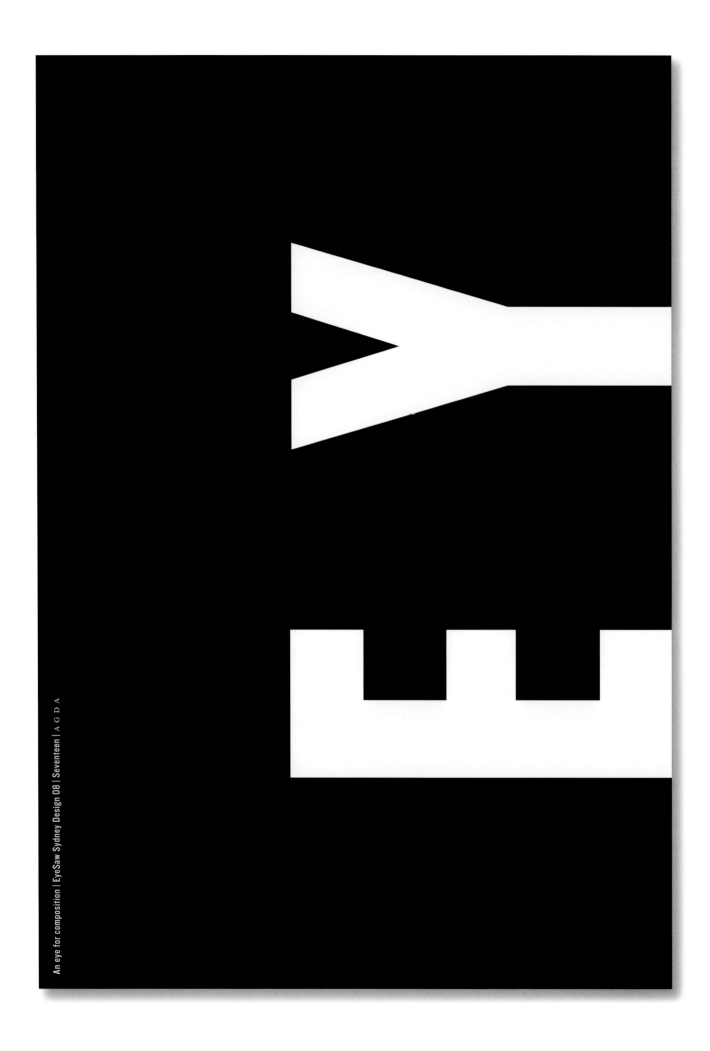

Post-War plastics:
Dieter Rams's innovations
in design, 1956 to 1974

11 September to
18 October 2008

72 Wigmore Street
London W1U 2SG

VITSŒ

neuarchitek tur

hitek tur

neuarchitek tur

düsseldorf, josef-gockeln-straße 9.

fachhochschule der ...max der ...

...im audi...nd: 8. februar,

diplomverleihu...

...uhr, fachhochschule düsseldorf,

2008.10 – 18 uhr, fachhochsch...

...tur: 7. februar

tag der offenen tür: 7. februar, 14 – 18 uhr, 8. februar, 11 – 20 uhr, 9. februar, 11 – 15 uhr, fachhochschule düsseldorf. *diplomverleihung: 7. februar, 19 uhr im robert-schumann-saal, ehrenhof 4 – 5, düsseldorf, diplomparty: 8. februar, 22 uhr, con-sum, ronsdorfer straße 77.*

diplomr undgan gkomm unika tionsde sign& produkt design

gestaltung: tristan schmitz, andreas uebele

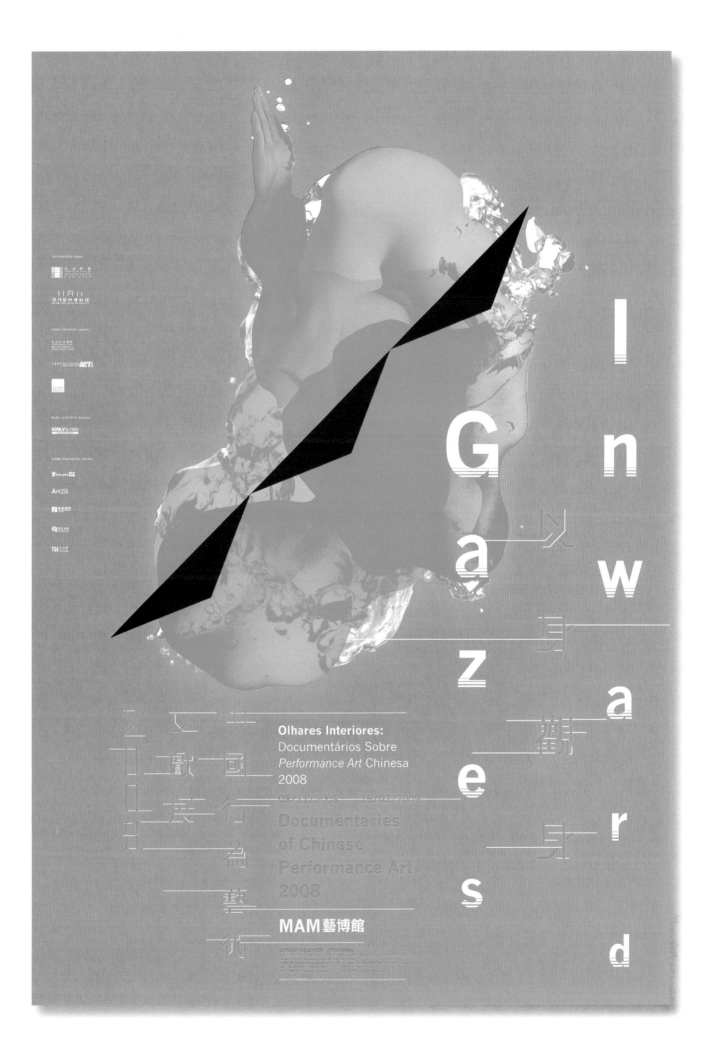

Olhares Interiores:
Documentários Sobre
Performance Art Chinesa
2008

Documentaries
of Chinese
Performance Art
2008

MAM藝博館

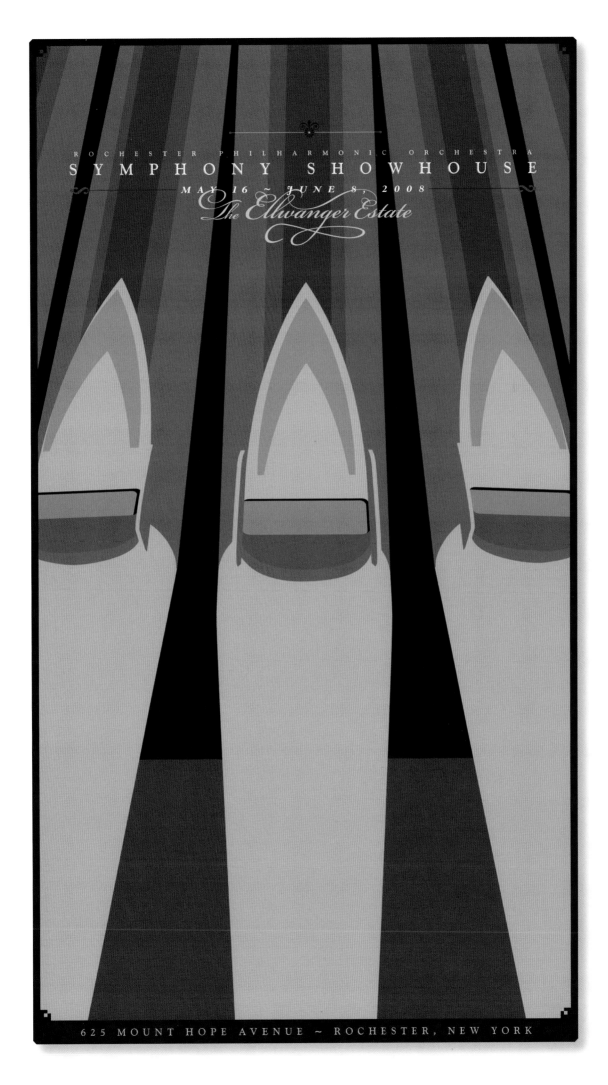

100

ART ISTS'

BOOKS

JANUARY 26–MAY 15, 2007

IN THE EARLY TWENTIETH CENTURY, ARTISTS BEGAN CHALLENGING ACCEPTED NOTIONS OF THE PURPOSE OF A BOOK. THEY SOUGHT TO TRANSFORM THE OBJECT FROM ITS LONGSTANDING STATUS AS A LINEAR CONVEYOR OF INFORMATION INTO A WORK OF ART. THE RESULT, A GENRE OF ART THAT CAN PUZZLE, AMUSE, AND CONFOUND VIEWERS, PLAYS OFF THE DUAL NATURE OF ARTISTS' BOOKS AS BOTH WORKS OF LITERATURE AND ART OBJECTS. *100 ARTISTS' BOOKS* HIGHLIGHTS WORKS FROM THE USC LIBRARIES' SPECIAL COLLECTIONS AND CELEBRATES THE DIZZYING ARRAY OF LITERARY SCULPTURES THAT ARTISTS HAVE CREATED, FROM THE SURREALIST EXPERIMENTS OF THE 1920S TO THE ONGOING EXPLORATIONS OF CONTEMPORARY PRACTITIONERS.

USC
UNIVERSITY
OF SOUTHERN
CALIFORNIA

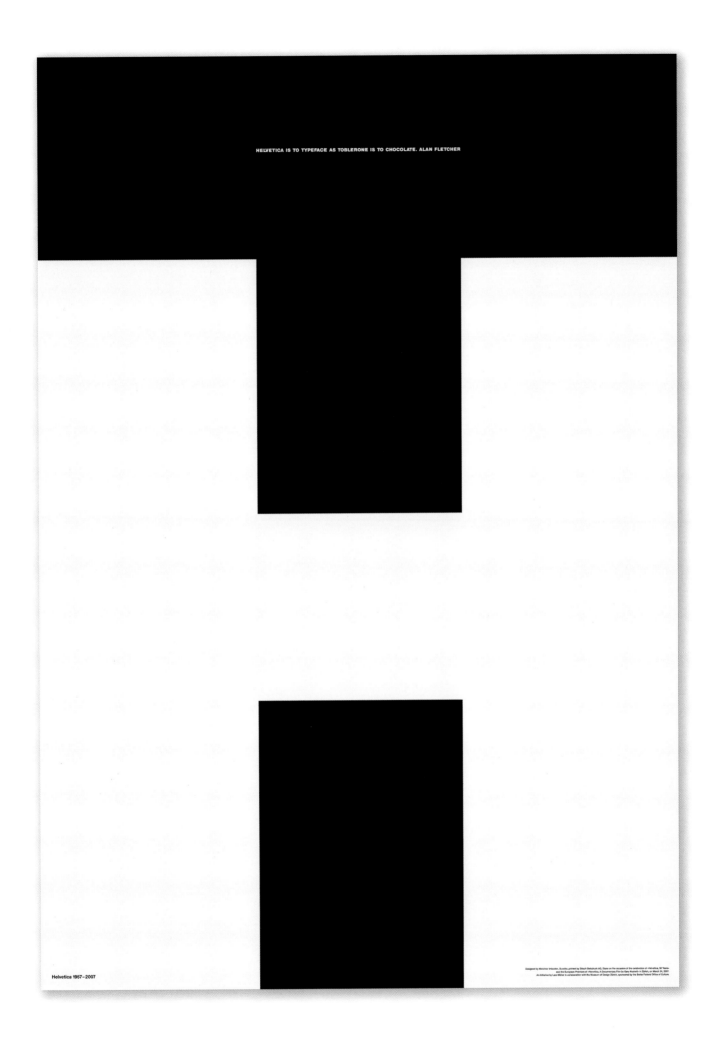

HELVETICA IS TO TYPEFACE AS TOBLERONE IS TO CHOCOLATE. ALAN FLETCHER

Helvetica 1957–2007

PLEATS
PLEASE

ISSEY MIYAKE

PLEATS PLEASE ISSEY MIYAKE   http://store.pleatsplease.com   AVAILABLE ON LINE, DELIVERY IN JAPAN ONLY
TOKYO = Place Minami-Aoyama 3-13-21 Minami-Aoyama, Minato-ku, Tokyo Phone : 03.5772.7750 ▪ PARIS = 201
Boulevard Saint Germain, 75007 Paris Phone : 01.45.48.10.44 = 3Bis Rue des Rosiers, 75004 Paris Phone : 01.40.29.99.66
▪ NEW YORK = 128 Wooster Street, New York, NY 10012 Phone : 212.226.3600 = tribeca ISSEY MIYAKE 119 Hudson Street,
New York, NY 10013 Phone : 212.226.0100 ▪ LONDON = 20 Brook Street, London W1K 5DE Phone : 020.7495.2306

PLEATS PLEASE ISSEY MIYAKE   http://store.pleatsplease.com   AVAILABLE ON LINE, DELIVERY IN JAPAN ONLY
TOKYO = Place Minami-Aoyama 3-13-21 Minami-Aoyama, Minato-ku, Tokyo Phone: 03.5772.7750 ▪ PARIS = 201
Boulevard Saint Germain, 75007 Paris Phone: 01.45.48.10.44 = 3Bis Rue des Rosiers, 75004 Paris Phone: 01.40.29.99.66
▪ NEW YORK = 128 Wooster Street, New York, NY 10012 Phone: 212.226.3600 = tribeca ISSEY MIYAKE 119 Hudson Street,
New York, NY 10013 Phone: 212.226.0100 ▪ LONDON = 20 Brook Street, London W1K 5DE Phone: 020.7495.2306

PLEATS PLEASE

ISSEY MIYAKE

PLEATS PLEASE ISSEY MIYAKE   http://store.pleatsplease.com   AVAILABLE ON LINE, DELIVERY IN JAPAN ONLY
TOKYO = Place Minami-Aoyama 3-13-21 Minami-Aoyama, Minato-ku, Tokyo Phone : 03.5772.7750 ▪ PARIS = 201
Boulevard Saint Germain, 75007 Paris Phone : 01.45.48.10.44 = 3Bis Rue des Rosiers, 75004 Paris Phone : 01.40.29.99.66
▪ NEW YORK = 128 Wooster Street, New York, NY 10012 Phone : 212.226.3600 = tribeca ISSEY MIYAKE 119 Hudson Street,
New York, NY 10013 Phone : 212.226.0100 ▪ LONDON = 20 Brook Street, London W1K 5DE Phone : 020.7495.2306

PLEATS PLEASE

ISSEY MIYAKE

PLEATS PLEASE ISSEY MIYAKE   http://store.pleatsplease.com   AVAILABLE ON LINE, DELIVERY IN JAPAN ONLY
TOKYO = Place Minami-Aoyama 3-13-21 Minami-Aoyama, Minato-ku, Tokyo Phone : 03.5772.7750 ▪ PARIS = 201
Boulevard Saint Germain, 75007 Paris Phone : 01.45.48.10.44 = 3Bis Rue des Rosiers, 75004 Paris Phone : 01.40.29.99.66
▪ NEW YORK = 128 Wooster Street, New York, NY 10012 Phone : 212.226.3600 = tribeca ISSEY MIYAKE 119 Hudson Street,
New York, NY 10013 Phone : 212.226.0100 ▪ LONDON = 20 Brook Street, London W1K 5DE Phone : 020.7495.2306

FRANCK MULLER

GENEVE

牛記茶室
外賣熱線 25455557

GOLDEN KIT
DRY CLEAN

"TWINS" BY JULIE SPEED

IGNITE YOUR IMAGINATION

TEXAS BOOK FESTIVAL

OCTOBER 28TH-31ST 2004 STATE CAPITOL, AUSTIN, TX

BENEFITING TEXAS PUBLIC LIBRARIES · FIRST LADY LAURA BUSH, HONORARY CHAIR

WWW.TEXASBOOKFESTIVAL.ORG

DESIGN BY SIBLEY/PETEET DESIGN, AUSTIN

BERGEN 8. – 15. OKTOBER 2008

FORFATTERSLEPPET

Nok en gang drysser forfatterne sine ville vekster ut over et bokhungrig publikum. Still deg i køen for å møte dem og ta på dem, lys levende! Forfattersleppet går av stabelen med brask og bram: forfattere i alle kategorier, fra de grønneste til de mest garvede, ser frem til å møte DEG. Tilfredsstill din hunger! Benytt denne enestående anledning til å meske seg med bokhøstens ferskvarer!

ARRANGØR: NORSK FORFATTERSENTRUM VESTLANDET

28 februari - 15 maart 2008

GOEB
BELS
FES
TIVAL

Koninklijk Conservatorium
Den Haag

Muziekgebouw aan 't IJ
Amsterdam

www.heinergoebbelsfestival.nl

ZAGREB FILM FESTIVAL
SC & KINO EUROPA, 19–25.10.2008, WWW.ZAGREBFILMFESTIVAL.COM

(Front)

Alliance
Graphique
Internationale

Chicago Congress 2008
September 23–27

Schedule of Events
September 24 – 27

September 24
Wednesday

September 25
Thursday

September 26
Friday

September 27
Saturday

Registration Information

www.agicongress.org.

Accommodations

AGI | sappi

(Back)

siff seattle international
film festival

may 22 thru june 15 2008   www.siff.net

512 **НОВЫЙ**

perspectives

新 NOUVEAU NUEVO NOUVEAU НОВЫЙ

NEW

siff seattle international film festival
may 22 thru june 15 2008   www.siff.net

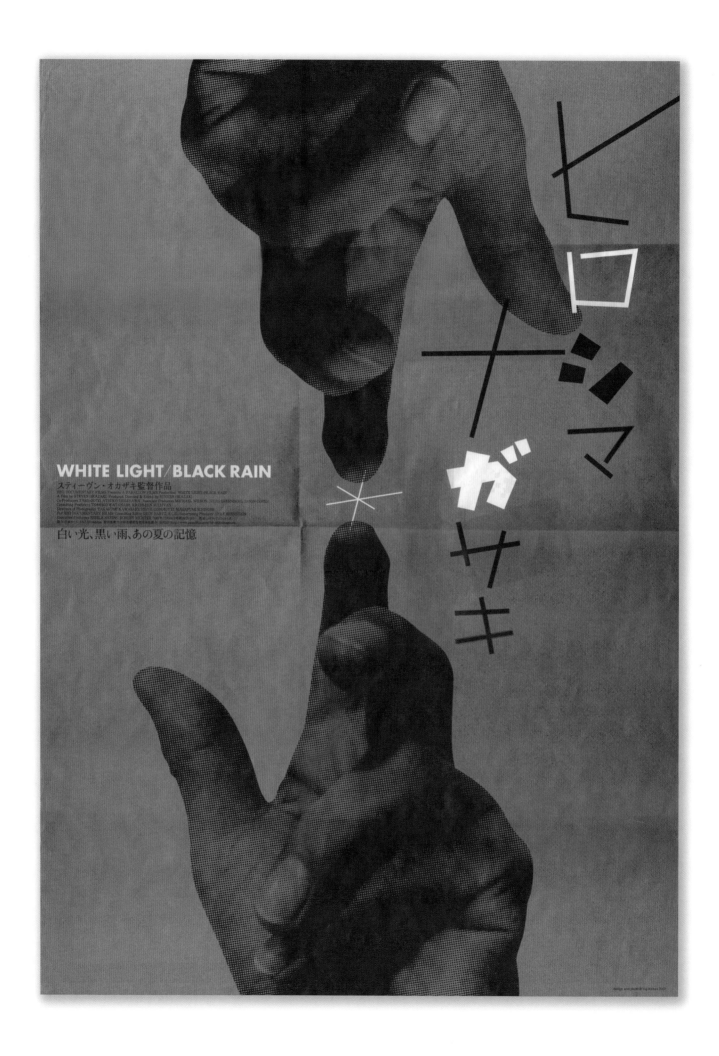

WHITE LIGHT／BLACK RAIN

スティーヴン・オカザキ監督作品

白い光、黒い雨、あの夏の記憶

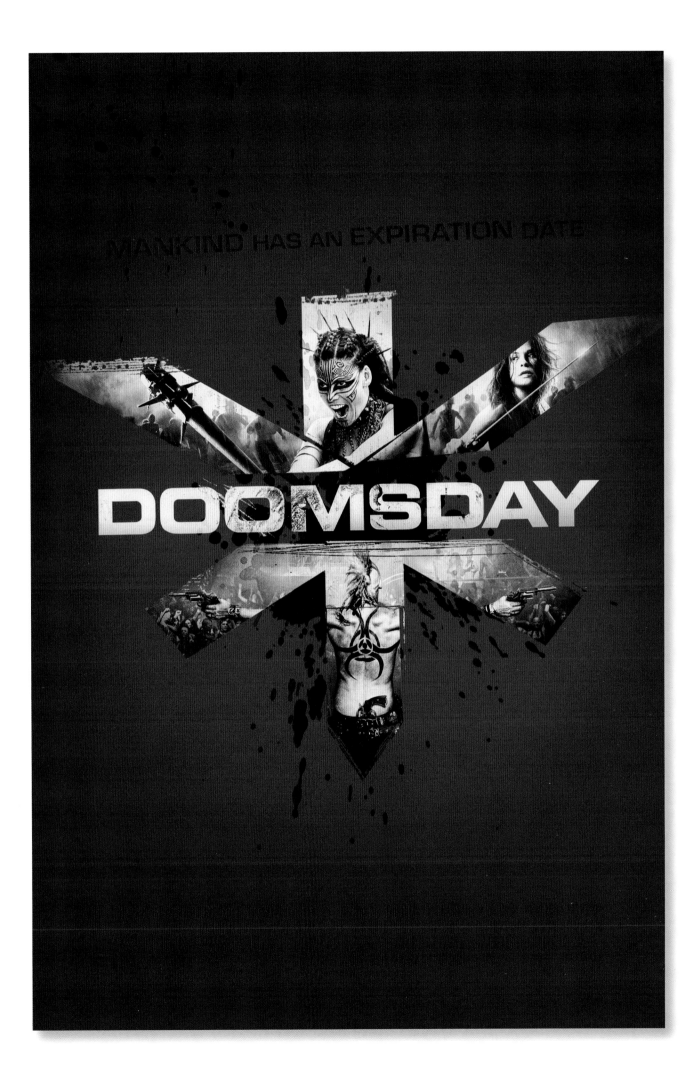

LOVE IS BLIND.
JULIANNE MOORE
BLINDNESS

CANNES 2008
OFFICIAL SELECTION
Opening Night

FALL 2008 ALLIANCE

BENDFILM :
a celebration of independent cinema

★ 4 SHORT DAYS THAT STICK WITH YOU ★

5th ANNUAL BENDFILM FESTIVAL |OCTOBER 9-12, 2008|

WWW.BENDFILM.ORG 541-388-FEST

Garbage Warrior

Turning trash into treasure

The fight
for sustainable
housing in a race
against time

A film by
Oliver Hodge

Hopscotch Films Presents
An Open Eye Media UK,
ITVS International and
Sundance Channel Presentation
"Garbage Warrior"
Music Composed and
Produced by Patrick Wilson
Editor Phil Reynolds
Executive Producer for
ITVS International Sally Jo Fifer
Executive Producer for
Open Eye Media UK Oliver Hodge
Producer Rachel Wexler
Filmed and Directed by Oliver Hodge
© Open Eye Media Ltd 2007

The ITVS International Media Development Fund
is supported by The Ford Foundation, The William
and Flora Hewlett Foundation and The John D. and
Catherine T. MacArthur Foundation A Co-Production of
open Eye Media UK, ITVS International and Sundance
Channel in association with The Documentary
Channel, YLE TV2 Documentaries and TV/2 Danmark.
This project has been enabled by Screen South and
the RIFE Lottery Funding Program.

www.hopscotchfilms.com.au

(M) Coarse Language

Something to eat, a place to sleep
& someone who gives a damn

A film about Homelessness

CANNONBALL
WINE COMPANY
HEALDSBURG, CALIFORNIA

www.drinkcannonball.com

ARTWORK/DESIGN COPYRIGHT 2007 MICHAEL SCHWAB STUDIO

ALWAYS FRESH

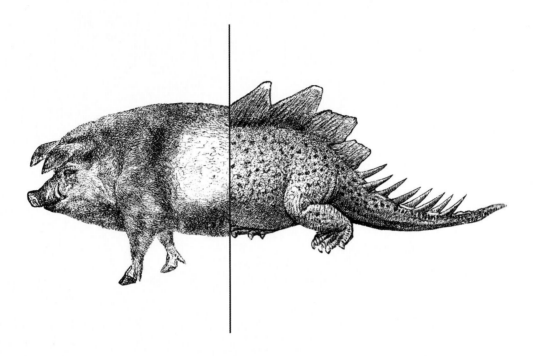

NEVER OLD

STUDLEY STORE
GREAT COUNTRY FOOD AND OTHER STUFF

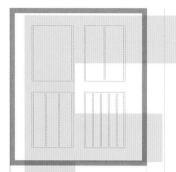

LAWRENCE SCARPA
pugh + scarpa, santa monica
art, architecture and landscape: the area where
overlapping systems and communities converge
WEDNESDAY, OCTOBER 1, 6:00 PM

MIDTERM PRESENTATIONS
MONDAY, OCTOBER 6-FRIDAY, OCTOBER 24, 2:00-6:00 PM
watt one, verle annis gallery, lindhurst architecture gallery

TROJAN PARENT WEEKEND
THURSDAY, OCTOBER 10-SUNDAY, OCTOBER 12

50 YEARS OF
THE ARCHITECTURAL GUILD
FRIDAY, OCTOBER 10, 1:00 PM
gin d. wong, faia conference center, harris hall
information: www.usc.edu/parent

GUILD PARENT'S RECEPTION
FRIDAY, OCTOBER 10, 3:00 PM
trojan courtyard, harris hall
information + rsvp: arcguild@usc.edu

NADER TEHRANI
office dA, boston
material pedagogies
THURSDAY, OCTOBER 16, 6:00 PM

2008 ACSA FALL CONFERENCE
MATERIAL MATTERS:
MAKING ARCHITECTURE
THURSDAY, OCTOBER 16-SUNDAY, OCTOBER 19
for more information visit: www.acsa-arch.org

USC ARCHITECTURE
IN ITALY, FRANCE
AND ASIA
verle annis gallery, lindhurst architecture gallery,
and rosendin atrium
MONDAY, OCTOBER 27-FRIDAY, NOVEMBER 7
RECEPTION: MONDAY, OCTOBER 27, 6:30 PM

USC ARCHITECTURAL GUILD
50TH ANNIVERSARY GALA
THURSDAY, OCTOBER 30, 6:30 PM
wallis annenberg building, (the armory) 1 exposition park
information + rsvp: 213 821 1845 or arcguild@usc.edu

WELCOME BACK
ALL SCHOOL MEETING
MONDAY, AUGUST 25, 12:00 PM
seely g. mudd auditorium, sgm 123

28TH ANNUAL USC
ARCHITECTURAL GUILD
GOLF TOURNAMENT
MONDAY, AUGUST 25, 10:30 AM CHECK-IN
lakeside golf club, toluca lake
information: 213 821 1845 or arcguild@usc.edu

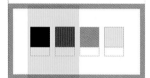

NABIH YOUSSEF LECTURE ON
STRUCTURAL DESIGN INNOVATION
GREG OTTO + TONY
MCLAUGHLIN
buro happold consulting engineers, inc.
architecture + engineering...a multi-disciplinary view: design
integration, system performance and sustainability
WEDNESDAY, SEPTEMBER 3, 6:00 PM

ARCHITECTURAL GUILD/
FACULTY EVENT
THURSDAY, SEPTEMBER 11, 7:00 PM
location TBA
information: 213 821 1845 or arcguild@usc.edu

VISIONS + VOICES:
THE USC ARTS AND HUMANITIES INITIATIVE
AI WEI WEI,
CHI PENG,
LIA JIAKUN,
QINGYUN MA
creativity at a crossroads:
art and architecture in china
WEDNESDAY, SEPTEMBER 17, 7:00 PM
bovard auditorium
www.usc.edu/dept/pubrel/visionsandvoices

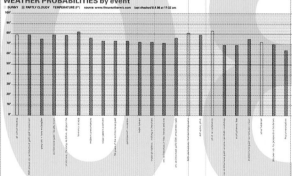

50TH ANNIVERSARY/
HOMECOMING EVENT
SATURDAY, NOVEMBER 1, TIME TBA
froehlich grove, adjacent to watt hall
information + rsvp: 213 821 1845 or arcguild@usc.edu

SUZANNE DEAL BOOTH AND DAVID G. BOOTH
LECTURE IN HISTORIC PRESERVATION
DELL UPTON, PH.D.
professor of architectural history, ucla
memorials to the second civil war: civil rights, urban politics,
and the geography of commemoration
WEDNESDAY, NOVEMBER 5, 6:00 PM

PH.D!A CONFERENCE
doctoral studies in architecture
THURSDAY, NOVEMBER 6
time + location: tba
information: 213 740 4589 or dnoble@usc.edu

USC ARCHITECTURAL GUILD
RESUME/PORTFOLIO WORKSHOP
MONDAY, NOVEMBER 10, 6:00 PM
gin d. wong, faia conference center and harris courtyard
information: 213 821 1845 or arcguild@usc.edu

SCOTT JOHNSON, FAIA
principal, johnson fain, los angeles
small and tall: the phantom of scale
WEDNESDAY, NOVEMBER 12, 6:00 PM

ARCHITECTURAL GUILD
SAN FRANCISCO MIXER
hosted by usc distinguished alumni
boris dramov, faia and bonnie fisher
FRIDAY, NOVEMBER 14
time + location: tba
information + rsvp: 213 821 1845 or arcguild@usc.edu

VISIONS + VOICES:
THE USC ARTS AND HUMANITIES INITIATIVE
YONA FRIEDMAN
irregular structures: conversations with yona friedman
WEDNESDAY, NOVEMBER 19, 7:00 PM
bovard auditorium
information: www.usc.edu/dept/pubrel/visionsandvoices

DISCOVER USC FOR PROSPECTIVE
FRESHMEN
SUNDAY, NOVEMBER 23, 10:00-4:00 PM
gin d. wong, faia conference center
information + rsvp: www.usc.edu/admevents

FINAL PRESENTATIONS
MONDAY, DECEMBER 1-WEDNESDAY, DECEMBER 17, 2:00-6:00 PM
watt one, verle annis gallery, lindhurst architecture gallery

WEATHER PROBABILITIES by event
SUNNY ▓ PARTLY CLOUDY TEMPERATURE (F°) source: www.theweathervio.com last checked 8.4.08 at 11:32 pm

UNIVERSITY OF SOUTHERN CALIFORNIA
SCHOOL OF ARCHITECTURE
WATT HALL 204
LOS ANGELES, CA 90089-0291

events requiring reservations and/or an admission fees are indicated with rsvp. all other events are
free and open to the public. unless otherwise noted, all lectures are on wednesday and begin at
6:00 pm and are held in the gin d. wong, faia conference center. usc architecture galleries are open
monday through friday, 10:00 am to 5:00 pm. for additional information please contact the usc
school of architecture at 213 740 2723 or visit our website at http://arch.usc.edu.

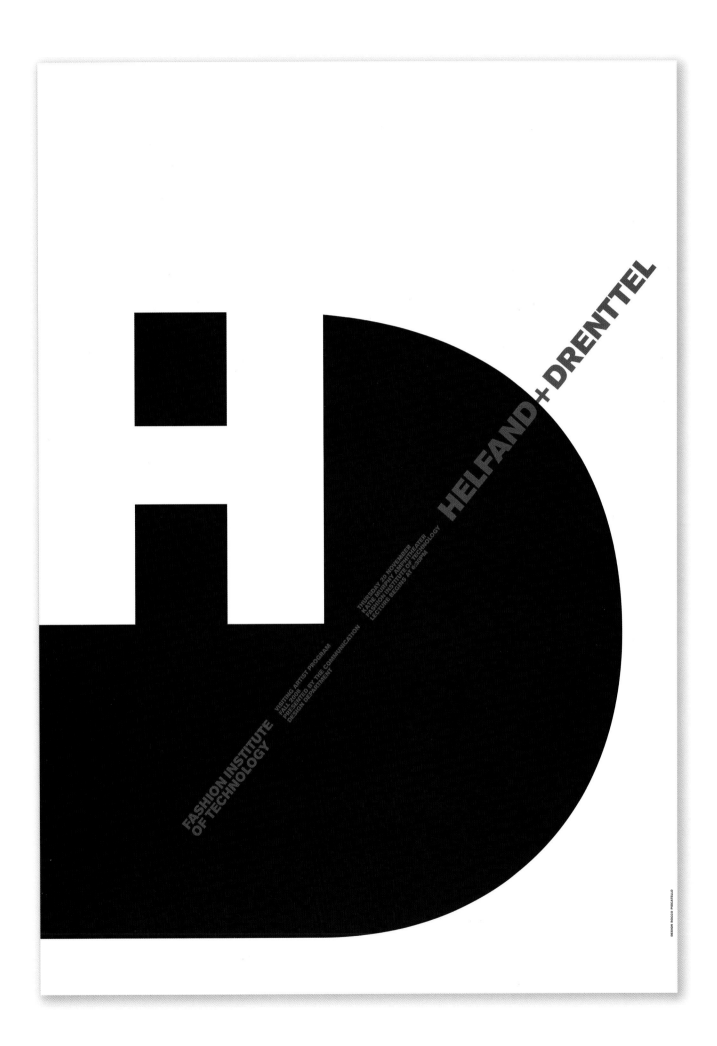

HELFAND+DRENTTEL

FASHION INSTITUTE OF TECHNOLOGY

VISITING ARTIST PROGRAM
FALL 2008
PRESENTED BY THE COMMUNICATION
DESIGN DEPARTMENT

THURSDAY 20 NOVEMBER
KATIE MURPHY AMPHITHEATER
FASHION INSTITUTE OF TECHNOLOGY
LECTURE BEGINS AT 6:30PM

DESIGN ROCCO PISCATELLO

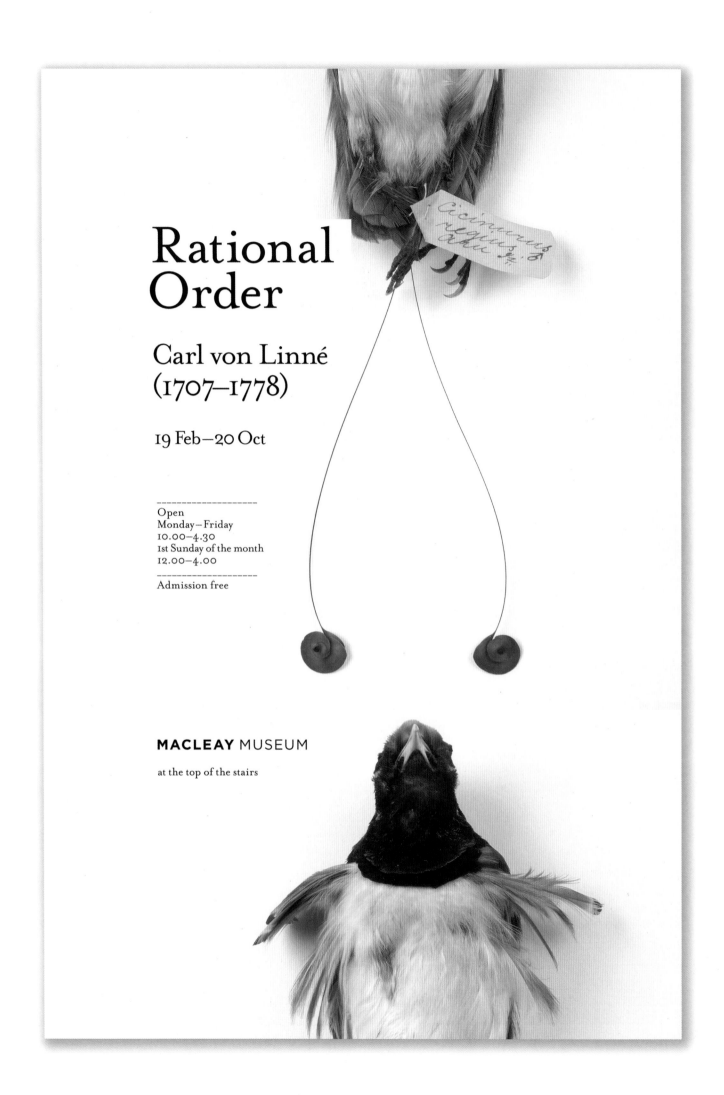

Rational Order

Carl von Linné (1707–1778)

19 Feb—20 Oct

Open
Monday—Friday
10.00—4.30
1st Sunday of the month
12.00—4.00

Admission free

MACLEAY MUSEUM

at the top of the stairs

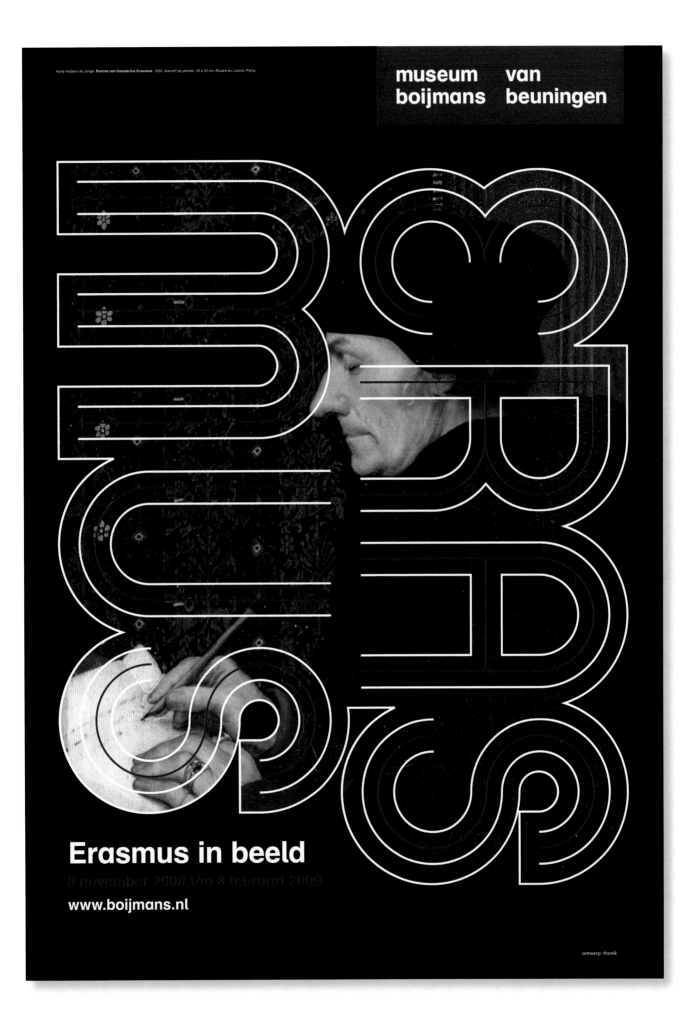

Hans Holbein de Jonge, **Portret van Desiderius Erasmus**, 1523, olieverf op paneel, 42 x 32 cm, Musée du Louvre, Parijs

museum van
boijmans beuningen

Erasmus in beeld
8 november 2008 t/m 8 februari 2009
www.boijmans.nl

ontwerp: thonik

MADISON MUSEUM OF CONTEMPORARY ART

DESIGNMMoCA

227 STATE STREET | APRIL 25, 26, 27, 2008

ART SHAPES INTERIOR DESIGN

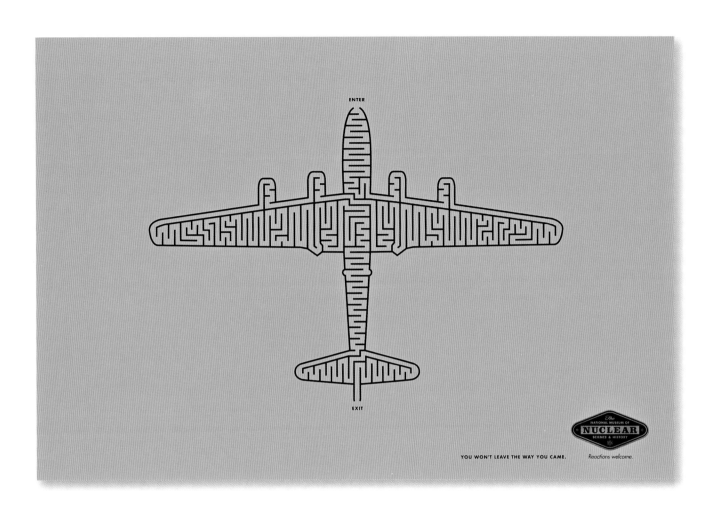

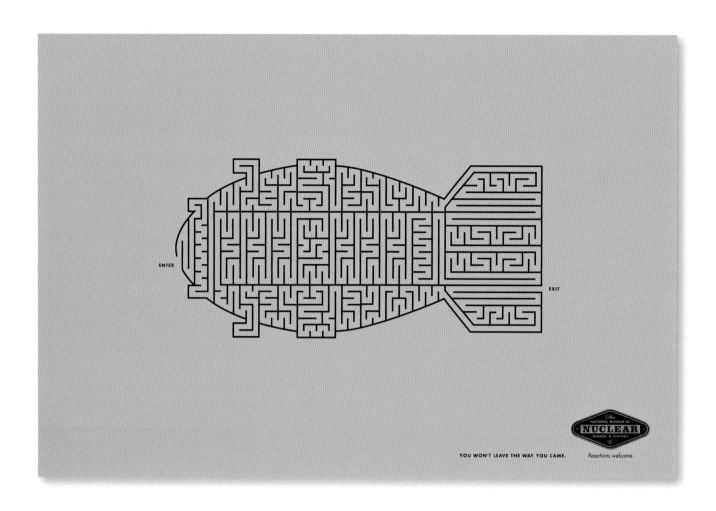

ENTER

EXIT

YOU WON'T LEAVE THE WAY YOU CAME.

Reactions welcome.

međunarodni dan muzeja
muzeji kao pokretači društvenih promjena i razvoja
international museum day
museums as agents of social change and development
18.05.2008
HMD

Die Münchner Secession

5. Juni bis
14. September 2008

Eine Ausstellung des
Museums Villa Stuck,
München

Museum Villa Stuck
Prinzregentenstr. 60
81675 München
www.villastuck.de

Öffnungszeiten:
Di bis So 11 bis 18 Uhr

Ein Museum der
Stadt München

M♥DICH
MÜNCHEN MAG DICH
850 JAHRE MÜNCHEN

SEC
ESS 1892
1914
ION

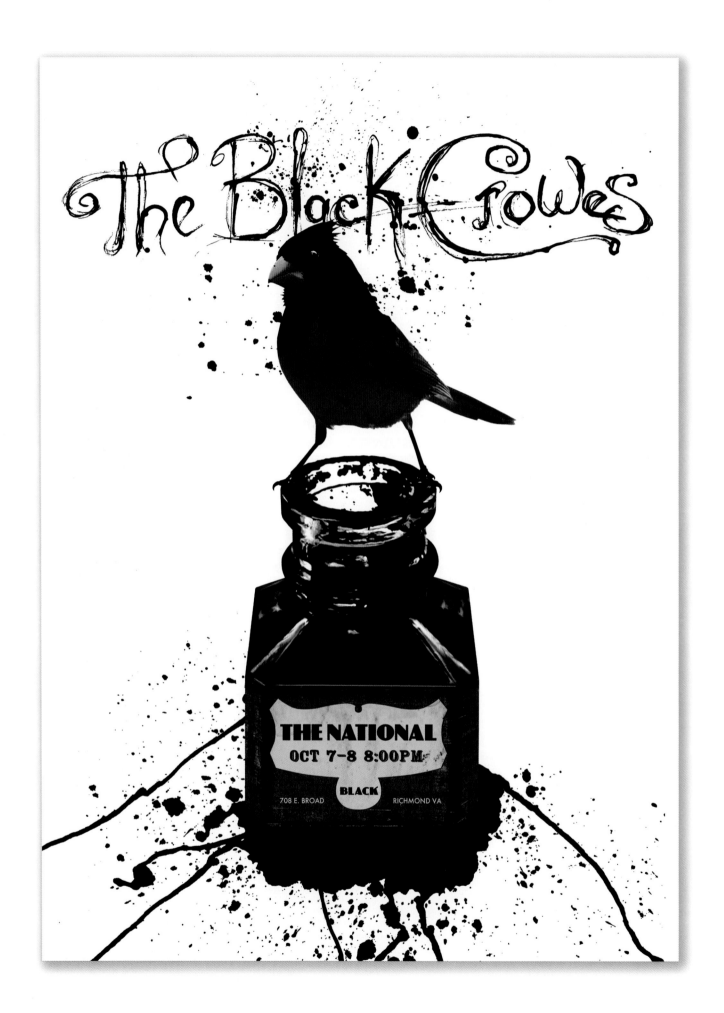

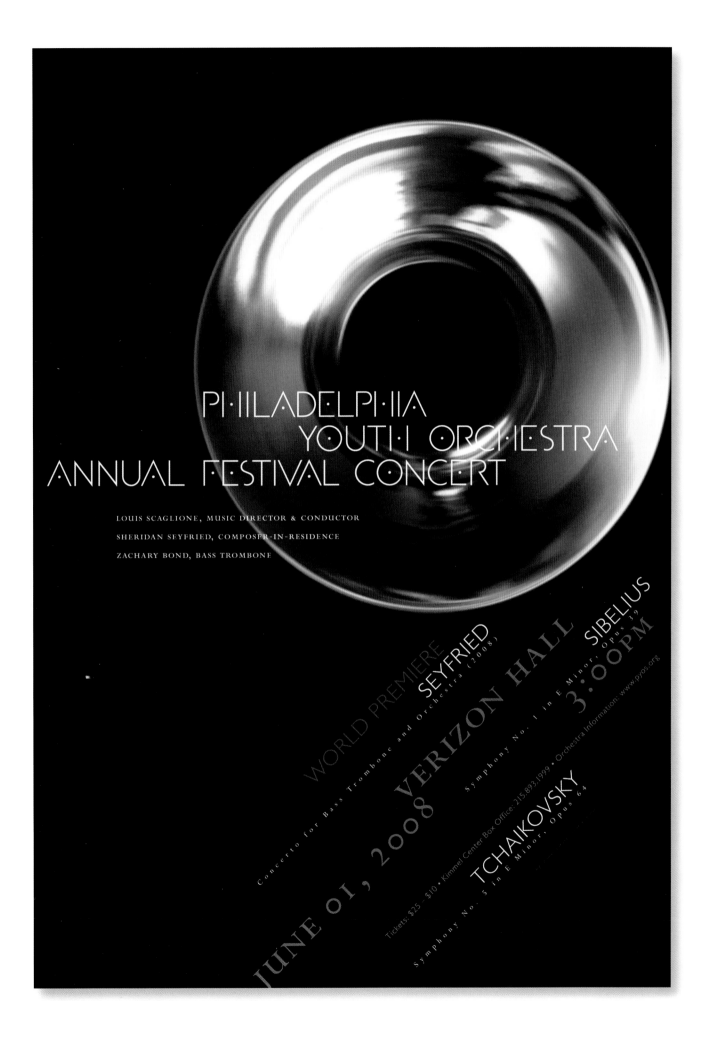

PHILADELPHIA
YOUTH ORCHESTRA
ANNUAL FESTIVAL CONCERT

LOUIS SCAGLIONE, MUSIC DIRECTOR & CONDUCTOR
SHERIDAN SEYFRIED, COMPOSER-IN-RESIDENCE
ZACHARY BOND, BASS TROMBONE

WORLD PREMIERE
SEYFRIED
Concerto for Bass Trombone and Orchestra (2008)

VERIZON HALL

SIBELIUS
Symphony No. 1 in E Minor, Opus 39

3:00PM

JUNE 01, 2008

Tickets: $25 - $10 • Kimmel Center Box Office: 215.893.1999 • Orchestra Information: www.pyos.org

TCHAIKOVSKY
Symphony No. 5 in E Minor, Opus 64

13 Ghosts / Sons of Roswell / Elliott McPherson / Bottletree / 1.5.08

QUART

JOUSIKVARTETIT RITARIHUONEELLA **2008 | 2009** STRÅKKVARTETTER PÅ RIDDARHUSET

Su 28.9 klo 18
aron-kvartetti
Eisler
Mozart
Korngold

Su 26.10 klo 18
Vertavo-kvartetti
Beethoven
Nielsen
Dvorak

Su 9.11. klo 18
Uusi Helsinki-kvartetti
& Christoffer Sundqvist, klarinetti
Mozart
Janacek
Brahms

Su 14.12. klo 18
Jousia-kvartetti
Mozart
Beethoven
Janacek

Su 25.1. klo 18
Guarneri-kvartetti
Beethoven

Su 22.2. klo 18
Kamus-kvartetti
Mozart
Wennäkoski
Schumann

Su 29.3. klo 18
Juilliard-kvartetti
Mendelssohn
Wernick
Ravel

Su 19.4. klo 18
Uusi Helsinki-kvartetti
Mozart:
E-P Salonen
Schumann

RITARIHUONE, RITARIKATU 1. LIPUT LIPPUPISTE JA OVELTA. BILJETTER LIPPUPISTE OCH VID DÖRREN. RIDDARHUSET, RIDDAREGATAN 1. **WWW.NEWHELSINKI.FI**

July 12 and 13
Hammachek Hall
Downtown Kewaunee
8 pm
Tickets
www.kewaunee.org

jazz ltd.

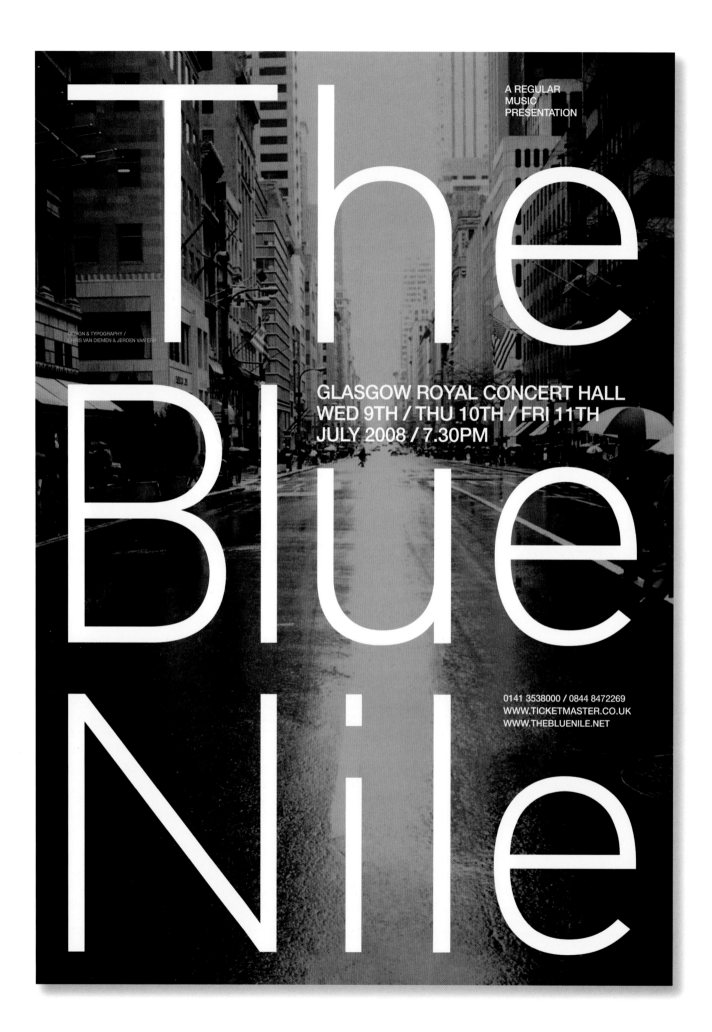

The Blue Nile

A REGULAR
MUSIC
PRESENTATION

DESIGN & TYPOGRAPHY /
CHRIS VAN DIEMEN & JEROEN VAN ERP

GLASGOW ROYAL CONCERT HALL
WED 9TH / THU 10TH / FRI 11TH
JULY 2008 / 7.30PM

0141 3538000 / 0844 8472269
WWW.TICKETMASTER.CO.UK
WWW.THEBLUENILE.NET

01.In the whale 02.Lotus
03.Anthem 04.The book
05.44077 06.Invisible man
07.Pablo 08.Rita
09.Yoni Rasetto 10.Gerbera
metro-ongen new album
in the whale 2007.11.14 out

Jazz i Willisau
Freitag, 29. Feb.
21.30 Foroom '08
Mark Helias'
Open
Loose
Mark Helias, b
Tony Malaby, s
Tom Rainey, dr

© 2008 Niklaus Troxler Willisau / Siebdruck Bösch AG, Stans

Jazz in Willisau Freitag 31. Oktober 2008 20.30 Foroom

Frank Möbus, g Rudi Mahall, bcl Oliver Steidle, dr

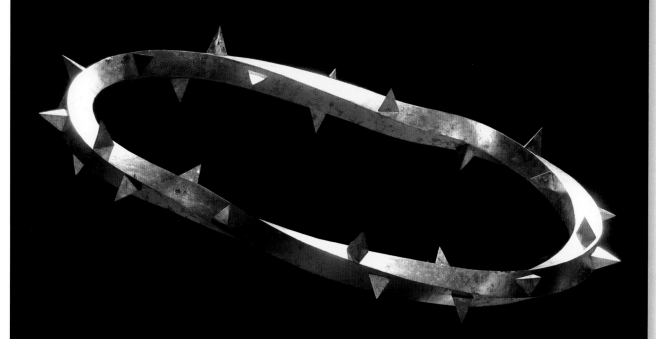

opernhaus zürich

modest MUSSORGSKIJ

BORIS GODUNOW

vladimir FEDOSEYEV   klaus michael GRÜBER   ellen HAMMER   eduardo ARROYO   bernard MICHEL   rudy SABOUNGHI   giuseppe FRIGENI   dominique BORRINI   jürg HÄMMERLI   CHOR und ORCHESTER der OPER ZÜRICH   Unterstützt von der Kühne-Stiftung

william **CHRISTIE** jens-daniel **HERZOG** nach einem Konzept von claus **GUTH** christian **SCHMIDT** ramses **SIGL** jürgen **HOFFMANN** **ORCHESTRA** „La Scintilla" der **OPER ZÜRICH** Unterstützt von der Vontobel-Stiftung und Ringier AG ab 15. **JUNI 2008**

georg friedrich **HÄNDEL**

RINALDO

OPERNHAUS ZÜRICH

OPERA THEATRE OF SAINT LOUIS

2008 SEASON   THE TALES OF HOFFMANN   MADAME BUTTERFLY   UNA COSA RARA   TROILUS AND CRESSIDA

DESIGNED BY TOKY BRANDING + DESIGN   UNDERWRITTEN BY CENTENE CORPORATION   ©2008 OPERA THEATRE OF SAINT LOUIS

+ CHRIS
SANDERS

[DRUMS OF WAR]

globalpeacenow.com

BEFORE

AFTER

CIVILIAN VICTIMS OF WAR HAVE A RIGHT TO QUALITY HEALTHCARE

HOMELAND SECURITY

Sichuan China Earthquake — May 12th, 2008

DOES RACE MAKE A DIFFERENCE?
Judge not by the color of his skin, but by the content of his character.

COLLATERAL
DAMAGE

Americans ... still
believe in an America
where anything's
possible — they just
don't think their
leaders do.

Barack Obama

Take Back America Speech
June 14, 2006
Washington, DC

"

If the **people
cannot trust** their
government to do
the job for which
it exists – to protect
them and to promote
their common welfare
– all else **is lost.**

Barack Obama

Speech at the University of Nairobi
August 27, 2006
Nairobi, Kenya

"

I am a strong believer
in the separation of
church and state...
But what I also think
is that we are under
obligation in public
life to **translate** our
**religious values into
moral terms that all
people can share,**
including those who
are not believers**.**

Barack Obama

CNN YouTube Democratic Debate
July 23, 2007
Charleston, SC

"

There is not a black
America and a white
America and latino
America and asian
America – there's the
**United States of
America.**

Barack Obama

Call to Renewal Keynote Address
June 28, 2006
Washington, DC

"

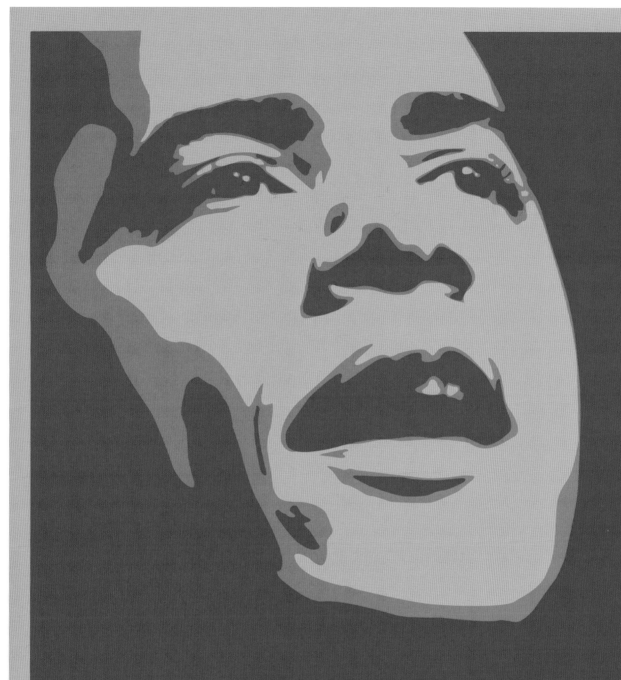

WE MADE
HISTORY

PRESIDENT OBAMA

BUSHED

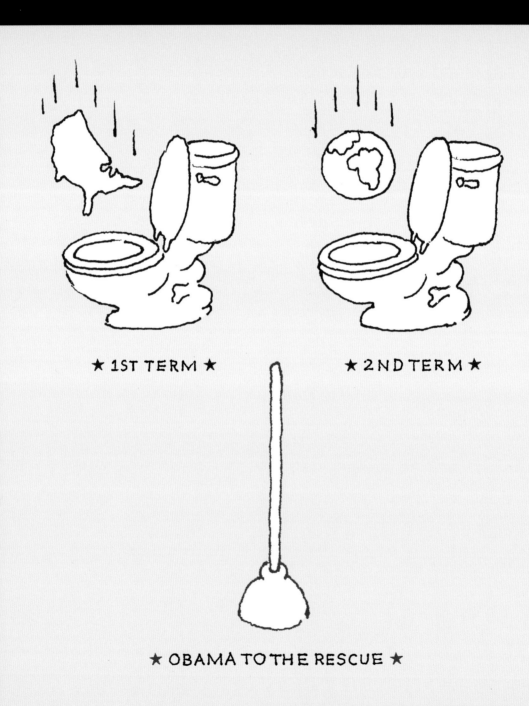

★ 1ST TERM ★   ★ 2ND TERM ★

★ OBAMA TO THE RESCUE ★

STEP STEP

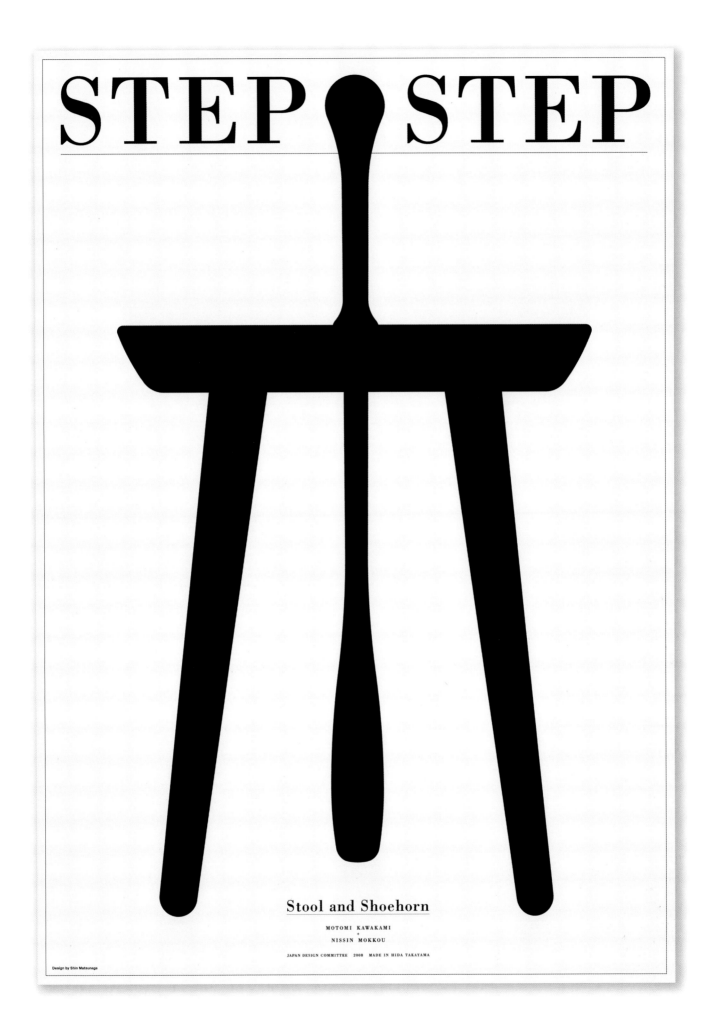

Stool and Shoehorn

MOTOMI KAWAKAMI
+
NISSIN MOKKOU

JAPAN DESIGN COMMITTEE   2008   MADE IN HIDA TAKAYAMA

Design by Shin Matsunaga

SPORE
by Jinny Blom

The first in a range of indoor and outdoor furniture by award-winning designer Jinny Blom. On view at Design Centre Chelsea Harbour, the set of three stools are made of a unique eco-friendly mouldable stone. They are cast to order and hand-finished in a small London workshop. For further information, please visit www.jinnyblom.com/spore

PHOTOGRAPHY BY TOM MANNION # DESIGN BY ROSE # PRINT BY PUSH

ONLY YOU
CAN RESCUE
THIRSTY CLIENTS

Just Add Water

AquaMark LX

Workaholic captured. Released back into wild.

"Making a disappearance", canoe on water, 7 days x 6 nights, 2008

Nowhere in particular is great this time of year.

The extended forecast calls for periods of peace followed by quiet.

ART

SERVING
CAPITALISM

FULLY CONNECTED

Our local knowledge is unrivalled across the region

breathing less gives
you a natural high...
so over the next few
years, as our air gets
more polluted with
each plastic bag we
use, with each drop
of gas we burn,
with each tree we
cut down, we will
soon be breathing
less...have fun
everyone!

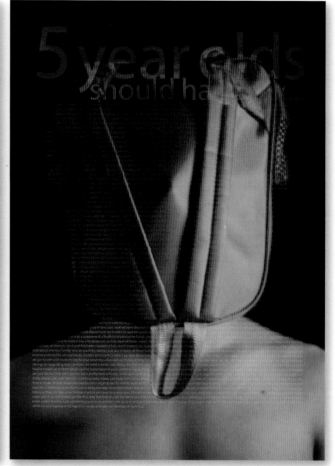

5 year olds
should have...

if you
ignore
past,
you
do
repeat
the
past
future
and
again...
again.

I work. 16 hours. a day. to pay

pedicures. her ha
ments. her cosmetic s
conversational english lesso
psychiatrist. her life coach. her
a private investigator. her lawyers.
zoloft. my penile implants. my pectoral implants. my
spray on body wax. my bleached teeth. my testosterone
injections. therapist. my psychologist my trainer. my life coach.
my lawyers. consultants. my priest. viagra. my retirement
fund. my life insurance. my gun.

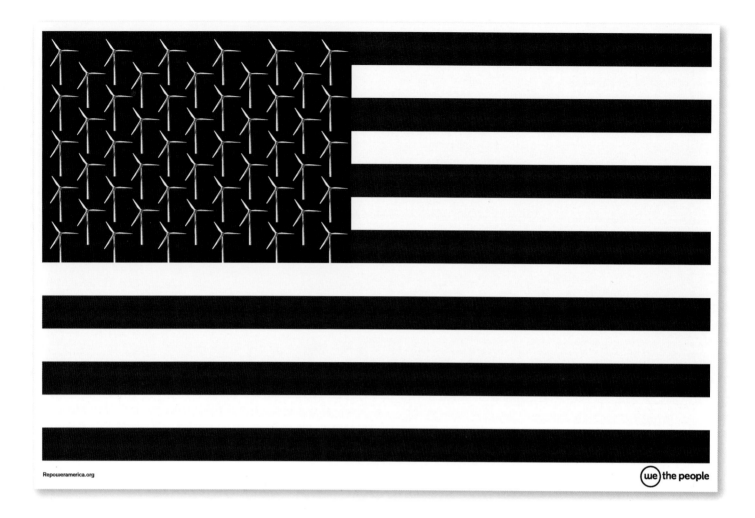

Repoweramerica.org

we the people

LOVE YOURSELF... PROTECT YOURSELF

USE YOUR HEAD — WEAR A CONDOM !

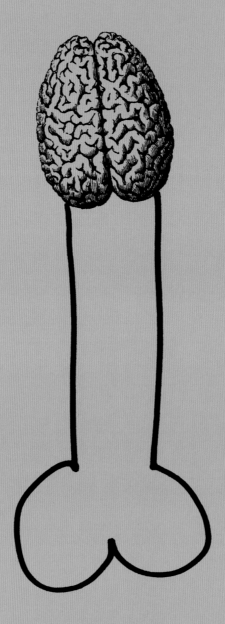

CONDOMS CAN PROTECT YOU FROM HIV AND SEXUALLY TRANSMITTED DISEASES.

KEEP YOUR CHILD OUT OF STREETCRIME
nogoingback.co.uk

**REFORM FOR LOAN SHARKS?
DON'T BUY IT.**

Payday lenders depend on trapping borrowers in a cycle of debt, rolling over the same loan again and again. It would be a felony for a bank to do business this way. But loopholes in the law have allowed payday lenders to get away with it for years, destroying livelihoods and decimating vulnerable communities.

STOP PREDATORY PAYDAY LENDERS
VOICE YOUR SUPPORT
919.313.8500

NEW TRICKS. SAME OLD SHARKS.

BLESS CHINA-
COMMEMORATION
OF
5.12
CHINA'S
MASSIVE
EARTHQUAKE

Ten years is all (we) have to cut carbon fuels.

Repoweramerica.org

Ten years is all (we) need.

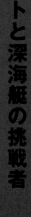

ロケットと深海艇の挑戦者

メタルカラーの時代 6

山根一眞

小学館文庫

わくわくする大科学の創造主

山根一眞

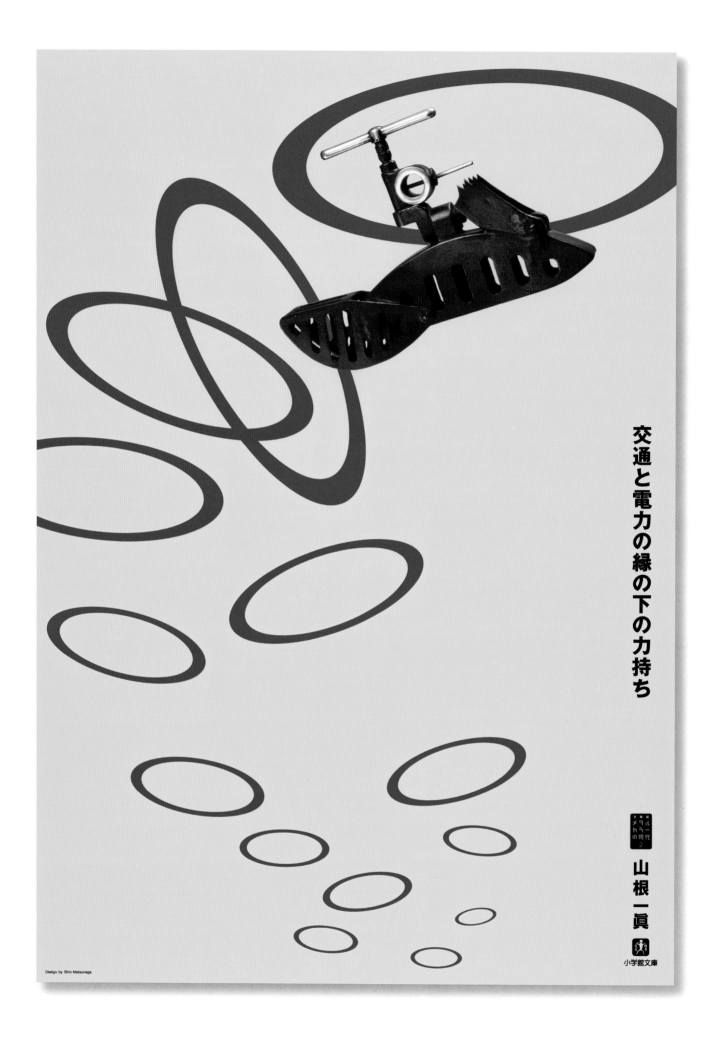

交通と電力の縁の下の力持ち

メタルカラーの時代2

山根一眞

小学館文庫

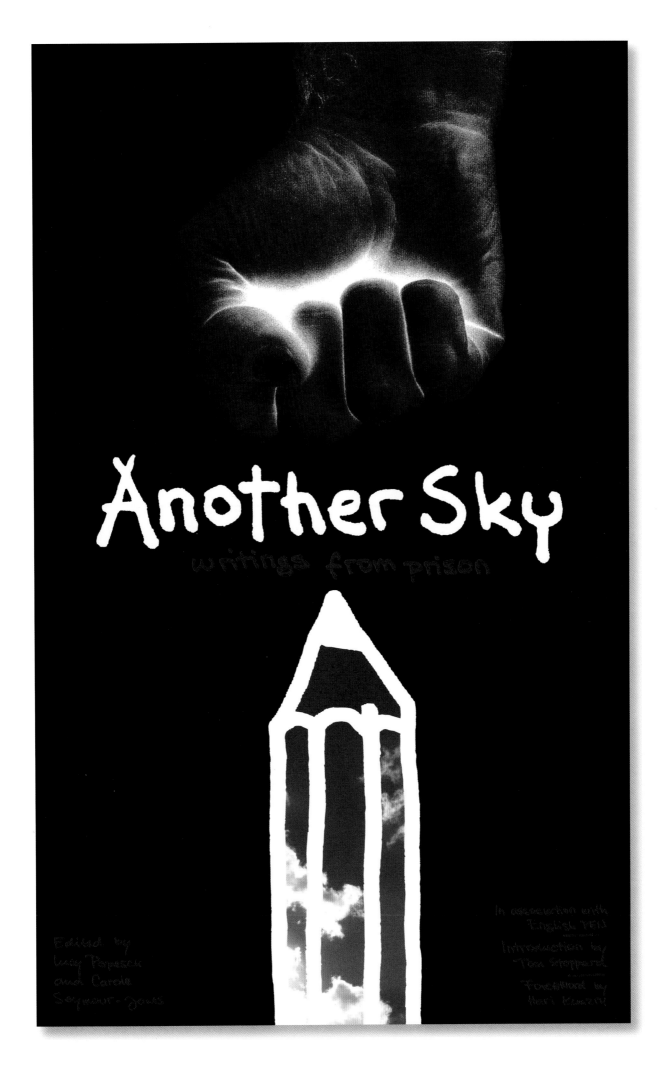

Another Sky

writings from prison

Edited by
Lucy Popescu
and Carole
Seymour-Jones

In association with
English PEN

Introduction by
Tom Stoppard

Foreword by
Henri Kuzni

DEFEND YOUR BASE

Tougher apparel starts with a tougher fabric.
DefendYourBase.com

CORDURA® baselayer

QUEEN
VICTORIA'S
MAKEOVER

———

Let the refurbishment begin.
Let the shopping continue.

———

QVB

PROBLEM

SOLUTION

Experience the unsinkable optimism of boating   SAILOR'S WORLD
sailorsworldmc.com

Team QUICK STEP   specialized.com

HENRIK **IBSEN**

in a new version by HELENE KVALE

A Doll's House

Director **Helene Kvale**

Designer **Mike Billings**
Costumes **Lucy Brown**

THE GENE FRANKEL THEATRE
24 Bond Street NEW YORK

Supported by The Marks Family
Endowment in Fine Arts

JUNE 6 - June 21
All Shows at **7:30**
also Sat & Sun Matinees 2:30
{ No show on Tuesdays }

THEATERMANIA
Tickets: theatermania.com / (212) 352-3101

b a t e d   b r e a t h   t h e a t r e   c o m p a n y

ROUGH PLAY PRODUCTIONS PRESENTS

KING LEAR

BY WILLIAM SHAKESPEARE
DIRECTED BY PAUL BUDRAITIS

NOVEMBER 6–30
THUR THRU SAT 8PM | SUN 7PM
NO SHOWS NOVEMBER 8TH & 27TH

THEATER 4 AT THE CENTER HOUSE
IN THE SEATTLE CENTER
NORTH ENTRANCE

Rough PLAY
PRODUCTIONS

INFO: ROUGHPLAYPRODUCTIONS.ORG | TICKETS: BROWNPAPERTICKETS.COM / 800.838.3006

BROWN PAPER TICKETS

SHAKESPEARE AS YOU LIKE

ARENA

PEKKA LOIRI | MAGENTA | 2008

UMBC
Theatre

Red Death

by Lisa D'Amour

directed by
Juanita Rockwell

Oct. 22 to Nov. 2
umbc.edu /arts

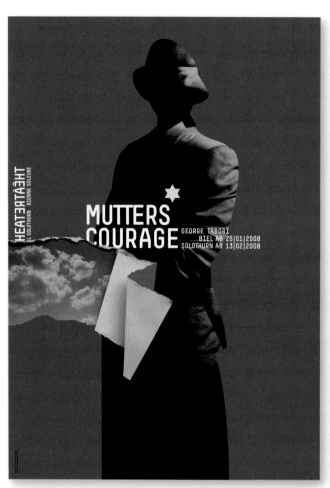

THEATERTHÉÂTRE
BIEL SOLOTHURN BIENNE SOLEURE

MUTTERS
COURAGE

GEORGE TABORI
BIEL AB 25|01|2008
SOLOTHURN AB 13|02|2008

THEATERTHÉÂTRE
BIEL SOLOTHURN BIENNE SOLEURE

BOCCACCIO
OPERETTE VON FRANZ VON SUPPÉ
BIENNE DÈS LE 21|12|2007
BIEL AB 21|12|2007
SOLOTHURN AB 27|12|2007

JOSEPH HAYDN

BIEL AB
12|09|2008
BIENNE DÈS LE
12|09|2008

SOLOTHURN AB
20|09|2008

L'ISOLA DISABITATA

THEATERTHÉÂTRE
BIEL SOLOTHURN BIENNE SOLEURE

ROMEO
UND
JULIA
AUF
DEM
DORFE

THEATERTHÉÂTRE
BIEL SOLOTHURN BIENNE SOLEURE

NACH DER NOVELLE VON
GOTTFRIED KELLER
SOLOTHURN AB 13|03|2008
BIEL AB 12|04|2008

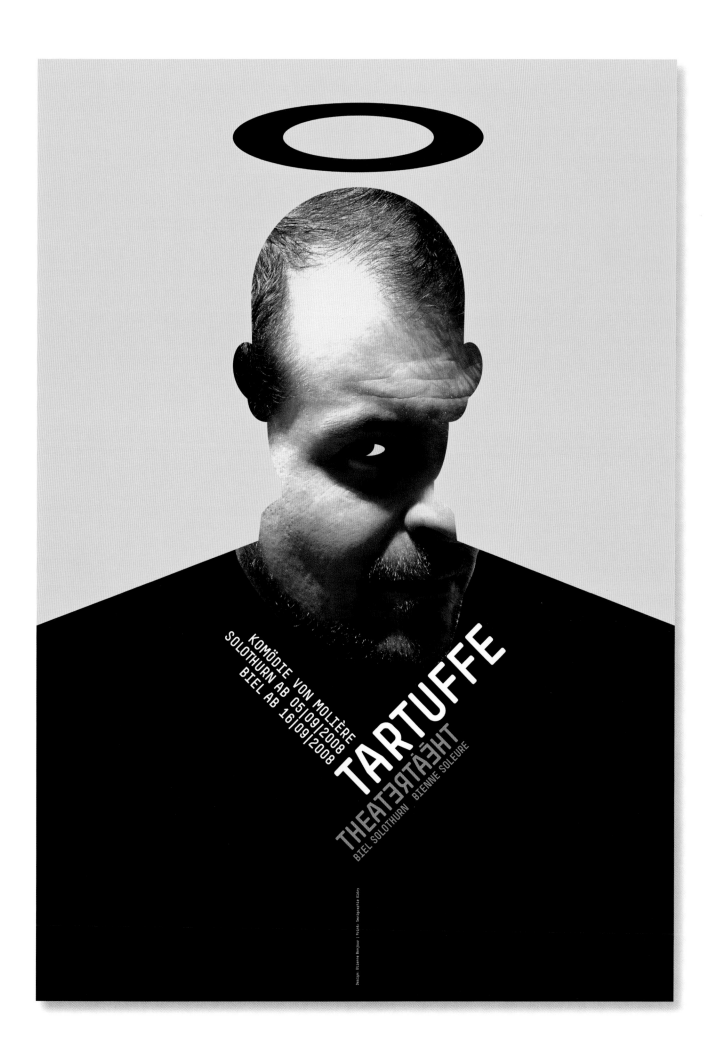

TARTUFFE

KOMÖDIE VON MOLIÈRE
SOLOTHURN AB 05|09|2008
BIEL AB 16|09|2008

THEATERTÄHT
BIEL SOLOTHURN · BIENNE SOLEURE

Design: Etienne Bonjour / Print: Serigraphie Uldry

Jil's 4th–5th Grade Class Presents

OLIVER TWIST

please sir...

the sleeper

university of wisconsin · green bay theatre performing arts presents

april **24** · **25** · **26** · **30** & may **1** · **2** · **3** at **7:30** pm · **Jean Weidner Theatre**

by **Catherine Butterfield** · tickets **465.2217** · directed by **John Mariano**

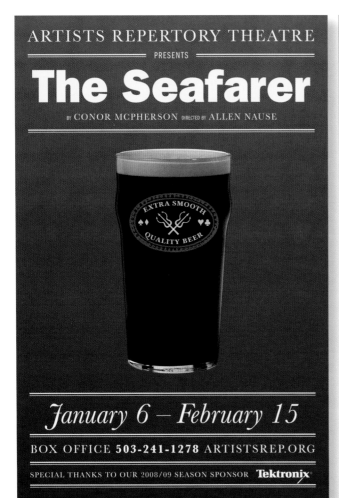

ARTISTS REPERTORY THEATRE
PRESENTS

The Seafarer

BY CONOR MCPHERSON DIRECTED BY ALLEN NAUSE

EXTRA SMOOTH
QUALITY BEER

January 6 – February 15

BOX OFFICE 503-241-1278 ARTISTSREP.ORG

SPECIAL THANKS TO OUR 2008/09 SEASON SPONSOR **Tektronix**

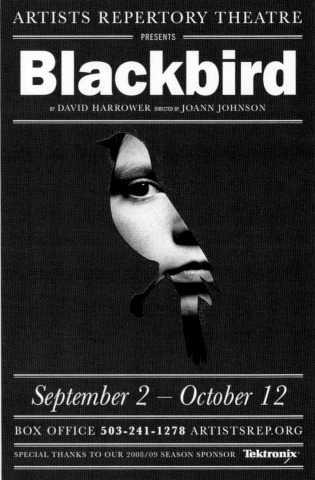

ARTISTS REPERTORY THEATRE
PRESENTS

Blackbird

BY DAVID HARROWER DIRECTED BY JOANN JOHNSON

September 2 – October 12

BOX OFFICE 503-241-1278 ARTISTSREP.ORG

SPECIAL THANKS TO OUR 2008/09 SEASON SPONSOR **Tektronix**

ARTISTS REPERTORY THEATRE
PRESENTS

Holidazed

BY MARC ACITO & C.S. WHITCOMB DIRECTED BY JON KRETZU

November 18 – December 28

BOX OFFICE 503-241-1278 ARTISTSREP.ORG

SPECIAL THANKS TO OUR 2008/09 SEASON SPONSOR **Tektronix**

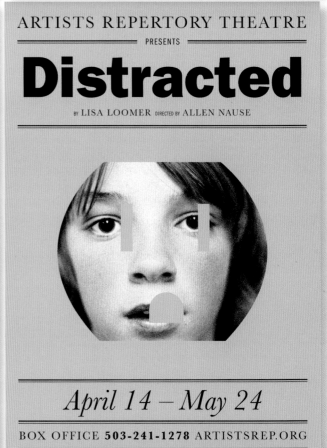

ARTISTS REPERTORY THEATRE
PRESENTS

Distracted

BY LISA LOOMER DIRECTED BY ALLEN NAUSE

April 14 – May 24

BOX OFFICE 503-241-1278 ARTISTSREP.ORG

SPECIAL THANKS TO OUR 2008/09 SEASON SPONSOR **Tektronix**

ARTISTS REPERTORY THEATRE

PRESENTS

Eurydice

BY SARAH RUHL DIRECTED BY RANDALL STUART

September 16 – October 26

BOX OFFICE **503-241-1278** ARTISTSREP.ORG

SPECIAL THANKS TO OUR 2008/09 SEASON SPONSOR **Tektronix**®

SAVAŞ İKİNCİ
PERDEDE
ÇIKACAK
YAZAN
OLDRICH DANEK
TÜRKÇESİ
REJİ
TASARIM
YÜCEL ERTEN
KOSTÜM
GÜLHAN KIRÇOVA
IŞIK
YAKUP ÇARTIK
MÜZİK
ÇİĞDEM ERKEN
KOREOGRAFİ
CİHAN YÖNTEM

İSTANBUL
DEVLET
TİYATROSU

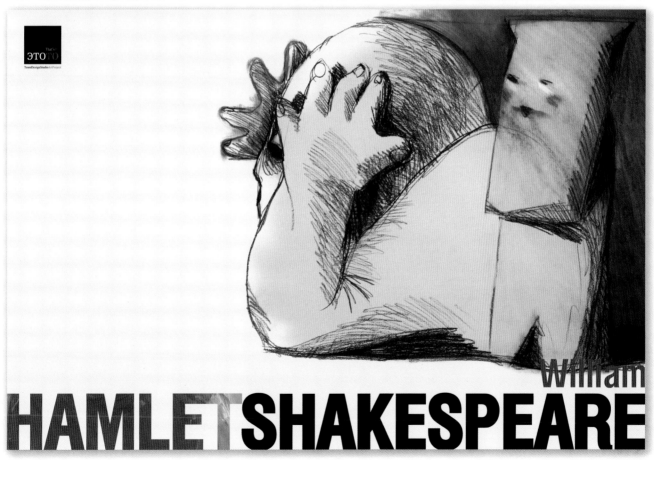

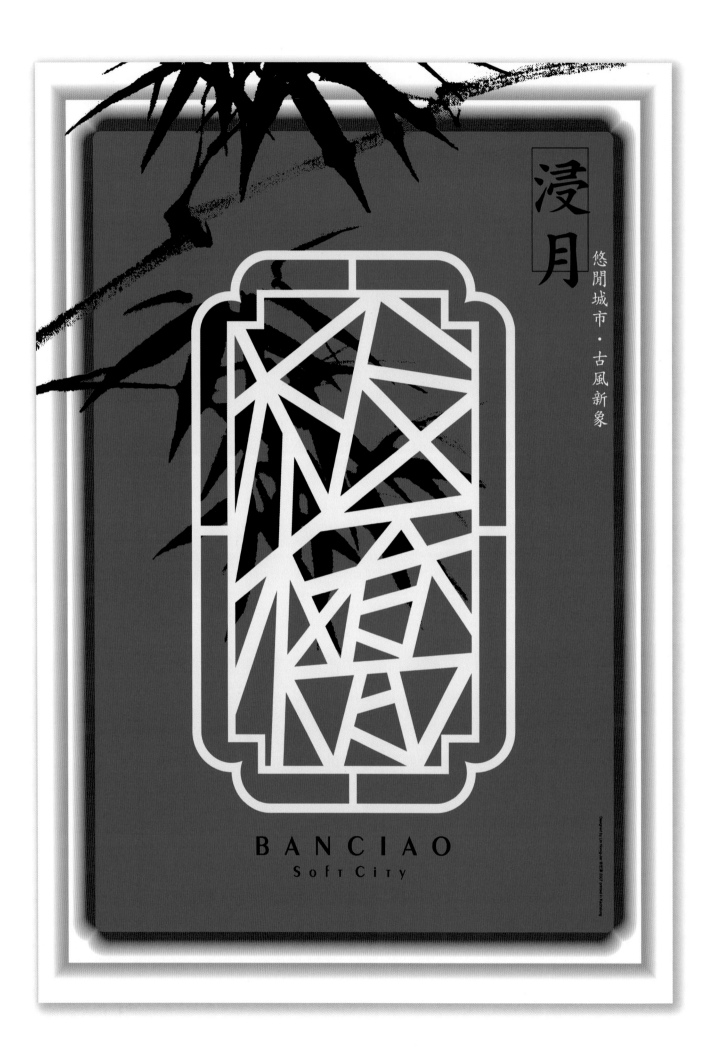

kewaunee

Harbor your dreams

Kewaunee Chamber of Commerce
308 North Main Street
Kewaunee Wisconsin 54216
1800 666 8214
www.kewaunee.org

UNBOUND
AT MAMMOTH

MICAH SHAPIRO
FRONTSIDE 720
MAMMOTH UNBOUND
TERRAIN PARK

04.21.08

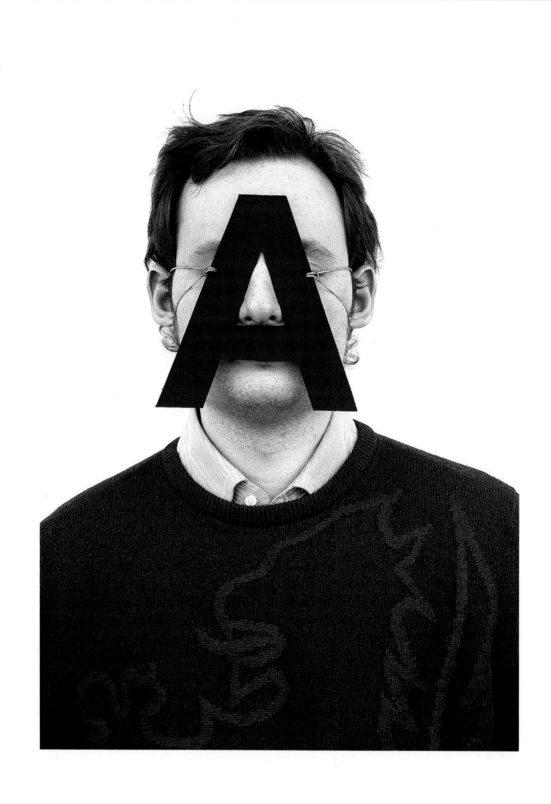

American Face

Chinese Face

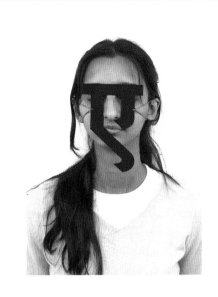

Indian Face

Korean Face

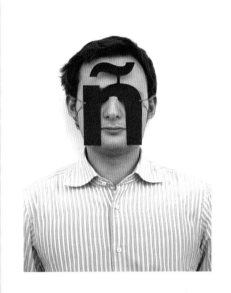

Spanish Face

Thai Face

Turkish Face

Japanese Face

w.al;ba
u!m t,a
n.zt g:r
ot;e.sk

FH D FB 2

tanzveranstaltung anlässlich des
22. bundestreffens forum typografie,
freitag, 23. februar 2007, 21.00 uhr.
fachhochschule düsseldorf,
josef-gockeln-straße 9, düsseldorf.

funk, hip hop und elektronische
rhythmen ermuntern zu avantgar-
distischer körperbewegung.

eintritt 7 euro, vorverkauf 5 euro.
kartenvorverkauf im carhartt shop
düsseldorf, mittelstraße 18 und in
der fachhochschule düsseldorf.

www.22ft.de

22. fo:r
;.um!ty
p-o?gr
.af,ie–

22. fo:r ;.um!ty p-o?gr .af,ie–

22. bundestreffen forum typografie – schriftgestalter über schrift und gestalten

23. bis 25. februar 2007 fachhochschule düsseldorf

frühbucherrabatt bis zum 31. dezember 2006

anmeldung unter www.22ft.de

prägende typografen sprechen über den schrift-entwurf und den entwurf mit schrift. die begleitende ausstellung »schriftgestal-ten« zeigt die entstehung ihrer arbeiten von der ersten skizze bis zur an-wendung.

mit vorträgen von philippe apeloig johannes bergerhausen hans rudolf bosshard dieter gorny luc(as) de groot hans-jürg hunziker paul van der laan uwe loesch georg salden fred smeijers kurt weidemann

eine veranstaltung der fachhochschule düsseldorf, fachbereich design, und des forums typografie e.v.

FH D FB 2   T.

"FOR HORSES TO GALLOP ON THIS LAND, THE VESTIGES OF MAN HAVE TO BE STILL FURTHER ERASED FROM THE EARTH AND THE SKY"

BİLGE KARASU, A QUOTATION FROM 'NIGHT'

Credits&Comments

Architecture

22 Not If Only When | Design Firm: Mende Design | Art Director: Jeremy Mende | Designers: Amadeo DeSouza, Jennifer Bagheri, Jeremy Mende | Photographer: Eduardo Solér | Print Producer: Donna Steger | Client: American Institute of Architects

23 GSAPP Events | Design Firm: Sagmeister, Inc. | Art Director: Stefan Sagmeister | Designers: Joe Shouldice, Richard The | Photographer: Mark Pernice | Client: Columbia Graduate School of Architecture, Planning, and Preservation

Comments: Columbia GSAPP has a history of folding their events poster in order to be mailed out. We took advantage of these contours and made a poster of a poster.

24 Stadion | Design Firm: Atelier Bundi | Artist, Art Director, Creative Director, Design Director, Designer, Typographer: Stephan Bundi | Printer: Seringraphie Uldry | Production Company: ArchitekturForum Bern | Client: ArchitekturForum Bern

Comments: For my "Stadium" poster I used various font styles of the letter "O". This letter reflects the shape of a stadium – a pitch surrounded by circular or oval-form seating. The overlaying of eight different letter forms symbolises the eight stadiums which were presented during this series of talks.

25 Lyceum 2008 | Design Firm: Skolos-Wedell | Creative Strategist, Typographer: Nancy Skolos | Designers: Nancy Skolos, Thomas Wedell | Executive Creative Strategist, Photographer, Set Designer&Props: Thomas Wedell | Printer: Serigraphie SSP Inc. Montreal Canada | Client: Lyceum Fellowship Committee

Comments: Annual Call for Entries for Student Architecture Competition.

26 Design Awards | Design Firm: Mende Design | Art Director: Jeremy Mende | Designers: Jennifer Bagheri, Amadeo DeSouza, Jeremy Mende | Print Producer: Donna Steger | Client: American Institute of Architects

Automotive

27 Wolf | Design Firm: WAX | Creative Director: Joe Hospodarec | Art Director: Joel Arbez | Copywriter: Sebastien Wilcox | Photographer: Philip Rostron | Client: Calgary Harley Davidson

Commemorative

28 Frida / Diego | Design Firm: Pirtle Design Inc. | Art Director: Woody Pirtle | Designer: Scarlet Duba | Client: Club de Banqueros de Mexico

Comments: Poster commemorating the 100th anniversary of the birth of Frida Kahlo and the 50th anniversary of the death of Diego Rivera, organized and exhibited throughout Mexico by the Club de Banqueros de Mexico. The poster was inspired by one of Frida Kahlo's paintings.

29 Cinanima 2208 | Design Firm: João Machado Design, Lda | Account Director, Art Director, Artist, Creative Director, Design Director, Designer, Illustrator: João Machado | Client: Cinanima

30 hope for sichuan | Design Firm: gggrafik-design | Art Director, Artist, Chief Creative Officer, Creative Director, Designer, Executive Creative Director, Illustrator, Typographer: Goetz Gramlich | Print Producer, Printer: Gerscher Druck | Production Company: gggrafik | Client: on my own

Comments: I was asked to contribute a poster for an exhibition concerning the victims of the horrible sichuan earthquake. i did research, and i saw that the panda bear is a symbol for the province sichuan. i also researched that the chrysantheme flower is a symbol for hope in dark times (cause its only flourish in autumn). so i mixed both impressions and integrate the font. ;) using black paper, white and laque silkscreen.

31 Kahlo Rivera 100 | Design Firm: Skolos-Wedell | Designers: Nancy Skolos, Thomas Wedell | Illustrator, Typographer: Nancy Skolos | Photographer, Set Designer&Props: Thomas Wedell | Client: Kahlo Rivera 100

Comments: Poster for Invitational: 100 Designers honoring Frida Kahlo and Diego Rivera 2008

32 A Creative Love | Design Firm: A2/SW/HK | Account Director, Art Director, Illustrator, Typographer: Henrik Kubel | Printer: MTA | Client: Frida Kahlo & Diego Rivera

33 Frida and Diego | Design Firm: Malcolm Grear Designers | Agency Producer: Malcolm Grear Designers | Designer, Typographer: Malcolm Grear | Printer: IO Labs Inc., Pawucket, RI | Client: The Fine Arts National Institute, Mexico

Comments: In honor of the 100th anniversary of the birth of Frida Kahlo and 50 years since Diego Rivera's death, The Fine Arts National Institute in Mexico organized a year-long celebration. An invitation went out to 100 world-known graphic designers who are members of the AGI (Alliance Graphique Internationale) to design a poster as an international visual homage to this iconic couple, Frida and Diego.

34 For Ever on Rise | Design Firm: Ashna Advertising | Agency Producer: Ashna Advertising | Art Director, Copywriter, Creative Director, Creative Strategist, Design Director, Designer, Typographer: Ladan Rezaei | Project Manager: Iraj Mirza Alikhani | Client: Kahrizak Charity Foundation

Comments: A poster to commemorate World Disabled Day.

35 World Industrial Design Day 2008 | Design Firm: Studio Uwe Loesch | Account Director: Henrik Kubel | Art Director, Designer: Uwe Loesch | Illustrator: Albrech Duerer | Printer: Color Druck Essen | Client: icsid International Council of Societies of Industrial Design

Communications

36 Reading - Compact Disc | Design Firm: HUGTOP Design Company | Art Director, Creative Director, Designer: Lin Horng-Jer | Client: Taiwan Poster Design Association

Competitions

37 **Platinum** Solidarity | Design Firm: Mark Gowing Design | Art Director, Creative Director, Designer, Photographer, Typographer: Mark Gowing | Printer: Mr Copy | Client: National Design Center

Comments: The Australian Nation Design Center runs a poster event each year called "The Australian Poster Annual". In 2008 the theme provided was the concept of Strength in Numbers. My poster was designed to embrace this ideal with an execution of the traditional solidarity poster theme. The knot of rope is made from smaller ropes, which are, in turn, made from smaller strands and smaller fibers. A metaphor for the people of the world coming together in strength.

38 NIKKEI BP ADVERTISING AWARDS 2008 | Design Firm: Shin Matsunaga Design Inc. | Art Director: Shin Matsunaga | Designer: Shinjiro Matsunaga | Client: Nikkei Business Publications, inc.

39 THE 22nd KOIZUMI INTERNATIONAL LIGHTING DESIGN COMPETITION FOR STUDENTS | Design Firm: Shin Matsunaga Design Inc. | Art Director: Shin Matsunaga | Designers: Shin Matsunaga, Kensuke Sakakibara | Client: Koizumi Lighting Technology Corporation

40 Corporations and Cities | Design Firm: Mind Design | Art Director: Niels Schrader, Amsterdam | Printer: Robstolk, Amsterdam | Client: Delft University of Technology in collaboration with the Berlage Institute, Rotterdam

Comments: 'Corporations and Cities' is an initiative of the Faculty of Architecture at the Delft University of Technology in collaboration with the Berlage Institute in Rotterdam that brings together international professionals, policy makers, researchers and scholars in the fields of corporate accommodation, real estate, organizational management, urban planning and architecture to consider the relations between urban planning and the accommodation of large-scale organizations. Just like urbanism tends towards the 'generic city', the visual identity for the 'Corporations and Cities' conference refuses the use of a static logo but emphasizes a modular design approach.

41 SOYA (Spirit of Youth Awards) | Design Firm: Frost Design | Creative Director: Vince Frost | Design Director, Typographer: Quan Payne | Project Manager: Laura Richardson | Client: SOYA (Spirit of Youth Awards)

Comments: The Qantas Spirit Of Youth Awards help Australia's new creative innovators to take on the world and their careers to the next level. Fashion designers, musicians, artists, photographers, visual communicators, object designers and filmmakers under 30 are invited to enter their work for the chance to win cash, Qantas flights and mentorships with leading lights of the international creative community. The Soya motion graphics were developed from the concept of seeing things from a creative perspective, standing out from the crowd and thinking big. The three dimensional typography and environment allow changing perspectives and motion to reveal information in a dynamic and immersive way. We created this years' campaign across all mediums including print, on-line, motion graphics and TV. Creative Director, Vince Frost, will also be SOYA's Visual Communications mentor for 2008.

42 The World's Smallest Poster Show | Design Firm: MINE™ | Art Director: Christopher Simmons | Designers: Christopher Simmons, Tim Belonax | Client: Poster Designers

Comments: The World's Smallest Poster Show: The world's Smallest Poster Show is an invitation-only exhibition of graphic work and posters from a San Francisco collector. Inspired by the title, we elected to produce a poster that was, itself, tiny. The result is a work that declares itself a poster while challenging the very format traditionally associated with that medium — an ideal provocation for the show itself.

43 AIGA 13 Show Call for Entries Poster | Design Firm: Fleishman-Hillard Creative | Account Director: Melinda Love | Art Director, Designer: Buck Smith | Client: St. Louis AIGA

Comments: The St. Louis AIGA 13 Show was to be held on Friday, the 13th. We wanted to use the ominous, bad luck association with that date in our call for entries poster. The poster became our interpretation of the back of a tarot card. The black, scuffed card uses a lot of creepy (and not so creepy) dingbats to complete our scary design.

Dance

44 Nutcracker 2008 | Design Firm: Paul Black Design | Art Director, Designer, Executive Creative Director, Illustrator: Paul Black | Client: Chamberlain Performing Arts

Comments: Consumer image champaign developed for the Nutcracker and part of an overall marketing effort.

45 Inuk2 | Design Firm: Frost Design | Creative Director: Vince Frost | Design Director: Anthony Donovan | Designer: Caroline Cox | Project Manager: Laura Richardson | Client: Sydney Dance Company

Comments: We worked with Regis Lansac's image of the dancers and created a themed poster based on set floor markings and clouds from the show, the type was also influenced by the markings on the set floor and is very organic in form. We created the show identity, campaign look and feel and applied to show collateral which includes poster, brochure, program and ads.

Designers

46 drs | Design Firm: Fabrique Communications & Design | Art Director: Rene Tonema | Copywriter: Hein Lobach | Designer: Chris van Diemen | Executive Creative Director: Jeroen van Erp | Illustrator: Chris van Diemen | Project Manager: Maartje Wensing | Client: Nancy Wulms

Comments: New Years Greeting: Fabrique in fifteen year – To the Future! Printed in ten different types of ink, this powerful greeting for the coming year shows the growth of the company. Fabrique's growing storing is told in fifteen layers and fifteen years. The growth is visible in diagrams and info graphics. Supported by a strong and continuous story, the poster shows the ever-expanding past until the present, with an eye on the future. You can see how many people were working there, how much food has been consumed, what projects have been done and what awards Fabrique has won, per year and in detail. The growth of all these figures sends one and the same message – To the Future! (Cheers). The posters were sent to clients and relations in a fancy envelope around the turning of the year.

47 Woody Pirtle / Anthropology Series #1 | Design Firm: Pirtle Design Inc. | Art Director, Illustrator: Woody Pirtle | Designer: Scarlet Duba | Client: Pirtle Design Inc.

Comments: The first in a series of 20 limited edition posters combining Victorian era portraits in combination with elements from Le Cabinet des curiosites naturelles.

Education

48 Art Center College of Design Poster | Design Firm: MIchael Schwab Studio | Designer, Illustrator: Michael Schwab | Client: Art Center College of Design

49 Platinum IDEA | Design Firm: SVIDesign | Designer, Illustrator, Photographer, Typographer: Sasha Vidakovic | Client: ALU Sarajevo

Comments: Poster for the lecture for design students depicting how to 'catch' the idea as a designer

50 "To Help See Possibilities" | Design Firm: Mirko Ilic Corp | Art Director: Michael J. Walsh | Creative Director: Anthony P. Rhodes | Designer: Mirko Ilic | Illustrator: Mirko Ilic Corp. | Client: School of Visual Arts

51 The Balancing Act | Design Firm: VSA Partners | Art Director, Designer: Michael Braley | Printer: Blanchette Press | Client: Portfolio Center

52 Media and Design | Design Firm: graphic communication laboratory | Art Director, Artist, Copywriter, Creative Director, Designer: Noriyuki Kasai | Client: Wako University Kasai laboratory

Comments: Notification poster of extension class.

53 Illustration Studies Tama Art University "Art" (Artery and vein) | Design Firm: Takashi Akiyama | Art Director, Designer, Illustrator: Takashi Akiyama | Client: Ilustration Studies, Tama Art University

Environment

54 Water for Life (a series of 3 posters) | Design Firm: João Machado Design, Lda | Account DIrector, Art Director, Artist, Creative Director, Design Director, Designer, Illustrator: João Machado | Client: João Machado

Comments: This series of posters has been especially created in order to alert the population for the need of water-saving.

55, 56 EVERYTHING IN THE RIGHT PLACE | Design Firm: Bisgrafic | Agency Producer, Copywriter, Designer: BISGRÀFIC | Photographer: FOTO-DISSENY J.E. | Client: RODA DE TER COUNCIL

Comments: The Roda de Ter Council's intention was to carry on encouraging the townspeople to leave their rubbish in the right kind of bin for selective collection and recycling, a system that had been started up a year before. So we cast around for an everyday image taken to absurd extremes, in order to show how easy it was to do what they were being asked to do: to put each kind of rubbish in the right place. The photo helped to achieve a sense of reality and of proximity to the people, thereby enhancing the message.

57 Ydinvapaa Merilappi | Design Firm: BOTH | Art Director, Designer, Executive Creative Director: Timo Berry | Creative Strategist: Kaisa Berry | Printer: Erweko | Client: Merilapin ydinverkosto

58 LOVE PEACE | Design Firm: Shima Design Office Inc. | Art Director, Designer: Takahiro Shima | Client: Takahiro Shima

59 SAVE THE NATURE | Design Firm: Shima Design Office Inc. | Art Director, Designer: Takahiro Shima | Client: Takahiro Shima

60 A lot of Garbage | Design Firm: Naughtyfish Design | Creative Director, Designer, Photographer: Paul Garbett | Client: National Design Centre, Melbourne

Comments: This poster was created as a response to the theme 'Strength in Numbers'. I documented the garbage that I threw out in a pretty average week.

61 "Jishin - Earthquake Japan" (Shinkansen) | Design Firm: Takashi Akiyama | Art Director, Designer, Illustrator: Takashi Akiyama | Client: Tama Art University

62 Healthy Water | Design Firm: Lank Graphic Design & Illustration | Art Director, Creative Director, Designer, Illustrator: Carina Lank | Client: Stockholms lansstyrelse

Comments: I made this Poster for "Stockholms lansstyrelse". It's made for an EU project called "Living Water", to gain attention for lakes and watercourses. They are working for cleaner water in the seas, rivers and lakes - a better environment for animals and persons, and for recreation (this is my second poster in this project). The Poster is silcscreened in five colours, 1000 ex.

63 CoRn | Design Firm: Texas State University-San Marcos | Art Directors, Designers: Jeffrey Davis, Claudia Röschmann | Associate Creative Director: Claudia Röschmann | Creative Director: William Meek | Typographer: Jeffrey Davis | Client: www.food-safe.org

Comments: As much as one fourth of all American agricultural lands raise genetically modified(GM) crops with little or no government oversight. Yet in most other countries, the same approach is subject to moratoriums,partially banned, or restricted with stiff legal penalties for non-compliance. Genetically modified foods contain substances that have never been a part of the human food supply. Keep our food as Mother Nature intended.

Events

64, 65 Design Austria Poster | Design Firm: Sagmeister, Inc. | Art Director: Stefan Sagmeister | Designer: Joe Shouldice | Photographer: Henry Leutwyler | Client: Design Austria

Comments: Two-sided poster for Stefan Sagmeister's lecture in Austria.

66 An experiment in collaboration | Design Firm: The Partners | Creative Director: Nick Eagleton | Designer: Emily Picot, Joe Russell | Client: The Jerwood Space

Comments: Brief – Design a catalogue to accompany an exhibition about the process of collaborative art.
Solution – Each visitor to the exhibition gets a huge printed poster and some simple instructions for cutting, folding and binding. The audience performs the final act of collaboration by using the poster to produce the exhibition catalogue themselves.
Result – 1000 posters, 1000 unique catalogues.

67 Design Firm: Doyle Partners | Art Director, Designer: Stephen Doyle | Printer: Enterprise | Project Manager: Rosemarie Turk | Client: Art Directors Club

68 40 | Design Firm: Rebeca Méndez Design | Art Director, Artist, Creative Director, Designer, Executive Creative Director, Photographer, Typographer: Rebeca Méndez | Client: Adam Eeuwens

Comments: This poster was created to announce a gathering to celebrate Mr. Eeuwens 40th birthday. This photograph of Mr. Eeuwens was taken a few weeks prior to the event at sunrise. The camera failed and created this 'transitional light'—neither day nor night, but an in-between—image, appropriate for the passage from 39 to 40.

69 The GRACE Greatest Generations Campaign | Design Firm: Palio | Account Director: Leah Warner | Agency Producer: Rick Bonnett | Art Director: Mike Lomanto | Associate Creative Director: Neall Currie | Chief Creative Officer: Guy Mastrion | Copywriter: Amanda Murphy | Creative Director: Paul Harrington | Ditital Artist/Multimedia: Alter Image | Printer: M&J | Photographer: Mark McCarty | Project Manager: Peter O'Toole | Client: inVentiv Communications

Comments: Through the use of iconic images such as Iwo Jima, First Man on the Moon, and Rosie the Riveter juxtaposed with images of elderly people struggling with modern day healthcare needs, the campaign sought to tug at the emotional heart strings of inVentiv employees encouraging them to donate to GRACE. The team successfully launched a multi-media campaign including print (postcards and posters), on-line (HTML e-mails and microsite) and video. To keep the campaign top of mind throughout the 4 week enrollment period, the team developed weekly e-mails showcasing the stories of our "heroes" lives and encouraging inVentiv employees to visit the microsite to learn more about our heroes lives.

70 Exhibitor Show 2009 | Design Firm: Vanderbyl Design | Art Director, Illustrator: Michael Vanderbyl | Designers: Michael Vanderbyl, Ellen Gould | Client: Exhibitor Magazine

Comments: 2009 Poster for the annual Exhibitor Show (exhibit trade show).

71 Playground of Fearless Thinkers | Design Firm: Vanderbyl Design | Art Director, Illustrator: Michael Vanderbyl | Designers: Michael Vanderbyl, Ellen Gould | Client: GRAVITY FREE

Comments: 2009 Poster for the annual Gravity Free Multidisciplinary Design Conference.

72 THE THIRD AGE WEEK | Design Firm: Bisgrafic | Account Director, Agency Producer, Designer, Illustrator: BISGRÀFIC | Client: RODA DE TER COUNCIL

Comments: An information poster on the Senior Citizens' Week, produced using an image which, though from our own time, draws its inspiration from Catalan poster design of the 1930s and 1940s, matching the age of the people involved. The main communicative notion is the number "3", alluding to the fact that this is the third edition, and that it is devoted to "the third age", i.e. people of retirement age.

73 beyondrisør – visual noise | Design Firm: bleed | Designer: Astrid Feldner | Project Manager: Frida Larsson | Client: beyondrisør

Commentary: Beyondrisør is a design conference that takes place every second year in Norway. The annual theme 2008 was "visual noise" (visuel støy) which was translated into typography. Cut letters, patterns, lines and pictures all mixed up together give a noisy but positive impression. The artwork was also used throughout the whole profile for the conference.

74 Keith Morris Lecture | Design Firm: Landor Associates | Art Director: Sam Pemberton | Copywriter, Creative Director: Jason Little | Designers: Sam Pemberton, Pan Yamboonruang | Executive Creative Director: Mike Staniford | Photographer: Pan Yamboonruang | Printer: The Production Factory | Set Designer & Props: Sam Pemberton | Typographer: Sam Pemberton | Client: Keith Morris

Comments: This poster was created for the typographer, Keith Morris, to promote his up coming talk. This was achieved through a typographic experiment that gave a witty nod to the speaker while complementing his trade. The key idea was a play on the title of the talk 'Keith Morris talks type over lunch'.

75 James Hackett Lecture | Design Firm: Landor Associates | Art Directors: Jason Little, Joao Peres, Sam Pemberton | Copywriters: Jason Little, Joao Peres | Creative DIrector: Jason Little | Designer, Illustrator, Typographer: Joao Peres | Executive Creative Director: Mike Staniford | Printer: The Production Factory | Client: James Hackett

Comments: For a lecture series where professionals from different industries present their craft, a poster was created to promote each speaker. The posters had to capture the individual essence of each speaker, hint at their topic area and cut through the visual clutter of a typical office environment. This was achieved through typographic experiments that gave a witty nod to each speaker while complementing their trade. The key idea for James Hackett, a motion graphics and broadcast designer, was to use the well known test card visual language to signify the talk broadcasting soon.

76 Promotion of Spanish books in China | Design Firm: CARRIO SANCHEZ LACASTA | Art Director, Creative Director, Designer: Carrio Sanchez Lacastal | Artist: Pep Carrio | Photographer: Enrique Cotarelo | Client: Spanish Minister of Culture

Comments: The image that heralds the presence of Spanish books in China is the result of a fusion between a book and a fan, fans of course being a cherished tradition in both countries.

77 Holy Cow Poster | Design Firm: Pentagram | Art Director: DJ Stout | Designer: Julie Savasky | Client: Pentagram

Comments: Self-promotion poster.

78, 79 80th Anniversary Posters | Design Firm: Jun Park | Agency Producer: Larid Christianson Advertising | Art Director: Mike Janowsky | Creative Director: Brad Osborn | Illustrator: Jun Park | Client: Laird Christianson Advertising/Hawaiian Airline

80 Booktoberfest | Design Firm: Crowly Webb and Associates | Account Director: Steve Molenda | Art Director: Pete Reiling | Copywriter: Liz Maimone | Creative Director: Jeff Pappalardo | Illustrator: Pete Reiling | Print Producer: Mary Kroll | Printer: Net W | Typographer: Crowley Webb | Client: Literacy Initiatives of Project Flight

81 Where Truth Lies | Design Firm: Visual Arts Press, Ltd. | Art Director: Michael J. Walsh | Creative Director: Anthony Rhodes | Designers: Michael J. Walsh, Brian E. Smith | Photographer: Harry Zernike | Client: School of Visual Arts

Comments: Poster / mailer designed for a School of Visual Arts sponsored event; a symposium on propaganda.

Credits&Comments

82 DSVC Kick-off Party | Design Firm: Range | Designer, Photographer: Garrett Owen | Printer: The Graphics Group | Client: Dallas Society of Visual Communications

83 Platinum Designerportraits Melchior Imboden | Design Firm: Melchoir Imboden | Designer, Photographer: Melchior Imboden | Production Company: Boesch Siebdruck Ag Stans | Client: Phoenix Gallery

Comments: An exhibiton which protraits Designers in two ways: photography and their own work. Melchior Imboden took the photographs on his journeys around the world during the last ten years.

Exhibitions

84 Erik A. Frandsen exhibition poster | Design Firm: Punktum design MDD | Agency Producer: Punktum design MDD | Artist: Erik A. Frandsen | Design Director, Designer: Søren Varming | Photographer: Ole Hein | Project Managers: Bjarne Bækgaard, Jens Erik Sørensen | Client: ARoS, Aarhus Artmuseum

Comments: Exhibition poster for a 3 month show abput the danish artist ERIK A. FRANDSEN and his show THE DOUBLE SPACE. The poster was made alongside an exhibition catalogue, and features a neon lamp overlayed with typographic anagrams made on the words in the artist name, thus explaining all the phasses that he has gone through in his career.

85, 86 Rising Water 1 | Design Firm: Taku Satoh Design Office Inc. | Art Director: Taku Satoh | Designers: Taku Satoh, Teppei Yuyama | Photographer: Tomotsu Fuji | Client: 21_21 DESIGN SIGHT

87, 88 Alles Gleich Schwer | Design Firm: Great Works | Account Director: Stefan Persson | Agency Producer: Great Works | Art Directors: Jacob Astrom, Jakob Nielsen | Creative Director: Ted Persson | Designer: Helmut Lang | Executive Creative Strategist: Magnus Walsien | Photographer: Elfie Semotan | Photographer's Assistant: Ditz Feyer | Project Manager: Jessica Thorelius | Client: ABSOLUT VODKA

Comments: These posters represent the collaborative campaign by ABSOLUT and Helmut Lang's of "Alles Gleich Schwer" . Helmut created a virtual interactive platform, in which art installations can live outside the physical and geographic space.

89 The Macao design biennale 07-08 | Design Firm: Joaquim Cheong Design | Art Director, Designer: Kuokwai Cheong | Client: Macao Designers Association

Comments: Seventh Biennial Design Macao's image is designed in three languages, Chinese, Portuguese and English as a basic element of a Chinese "Plum Blossom" style arena, won the race is not easy.

90 MESATEX JAPAN FABRIC COLLECTION | Design Firm: 702 Design Works | Account Director, Art Director, Design Director: Gaku Ohsugi | Designer: Tadashi Kobayashi | Production Company: 702 Design Works | Client: MESATEX JAPAN

Comments: These 3 posters were made for an exhibition of Fall and Winter curtain collection of a fabric company, Mesatex Japan.

91 MESATEX JAPAN FABRIC 2008 | Design Firm: 702 Design Works | Account Director, Art Director, Design Director: Gaku Ohsugi | Designer: Yuriko Matsumura | Production Company: 702 Design Works | Client: MESATEX JAPAN

Comments: This poster was made for an exhibition of curtain and lace of a fabric company, Mesatex Japan.

92, 93 Brno Echo: Ornament and Crime from Adolf Loos to Now | Design Firm: Pentagram | Designer: Abbott Miller | Client: The Moravian Gallery

Comments: "Brno Echo: Ornament and Crime from Adolf Loos to Now" was a design exhibition curated and designed by Abbott Miller and held in conjunction with the 23rd International Biennial of Graphic Design Brno, one of Europe's largest festivals of graphic design. "Brno Echo" staged a lively dialogue between historical and contemporary design around the subject of modern ornament. Adolf Loos' 1908 manifesto "Ornament and Crime" served as the conceptual foundation for the exhibition that looked at the recurrence of concentric lines and patterns that constitute a fundamental grammar of modern ornament, connecting everything from the Wiener Werkstätte through Pop Art to current variants of retro-futurism. For the exhibition, Miller designed a series of four posters built from the "B" Jiri Hadlac designed for the original Biennial identity in 1964. The posters utilize that letterform to create the full phrase BRNO ECHO. The posters were silkscreened for a deep color saturation that gives them an unmistakable look and feel.

94 Missverständnisse – Stolpersteine der Kommunikation (Misunderstandings – Stumbling Blocks of Communication) | Design Firm: Pentagram Design Ltd. | Art Director: Justus Oehler | Designer: Justus Oehler, Christiane Weismueller | Client: Museum of Communication Germany

Comments: Pentagram has designed the catalogue and campaign for Missverständnisse–Stolpersteine der Kommunikation (Misunderstandings–Stumbling Blocks of Communication), an exhibition at the Museum of Communication in Germany. Misunderstandings are part of our daily lives, and the exhibition explores when and how they occur and the funny episodes or unexpected consequences they cause. The exhibition poster and graphics communicate the topic by using illustrations of homonyms, or words with two or more meanings, such as a boxer (athlete) and a boxer (dog). The Misunderstandings exhibition poster therefore shows a faucet and a rooster- both share the same word in German, Hahn.

95 Exhibition Posters | Design Firm: Pentagram Design Ltd., Berlin | Art Director: Justus Oehler | Designers: Justus Oehler, Josephine Rank | Client: Deutsche Kinemathek – Museum für Film und Fernsehen

Comments: This is a series of 5 exhibition posters designed for the Deutsche Kinemathek — Museum für Film und Fernsehen (German Museum of Film and Television) in Berlin. Located at the Potsdamer Platz, in the heart of the city, the museum celebrates Germany's contribution to world cinema and is comparable to institutions like the British Film Institute in London and the Cinémathèque Française in Paris. Holdings from Marlene Dietrich's estate form the core of the permanent collection. The museum was formerly named the Filmmuseum Berlin, but relaunched recently with a parallel focus on television. It needed an identity that would reflect both media, and the new logo, designed by Pentagram, features two screens intersecting to form a silvery-grey letter "M. The design of the posters therefore pursues the identity by using diagonals as main design elements.
Posters:
1. Poster for the museum's 2008 homage to the Italian filmmaker Francesco Rosi.
2. Poster for the film series In the talkies every Sunday night: Sound-Film-Music, 1929-1933.
3. Luis Buñuel retrospective poster.
4. 100 years German film history
5. Ulrike Ottinger exhibition poster

96 EyeSaw | Design Firm: Landor Associates | Art Director, Copywriter: Jason Little | Creative Director: Jason Little | Designers: Jason Little, Joao Peres, Ivana Martinovic, Pan Yamboonruang, Sam Pemberton, Angela McCarthy | Executive Creative Director: Mike Staniford | Illustrator: Joao Peres | Printer: Wizardy | Typographer: Jason Little, Joao Peres | Client: AGDA / Sydney Design '08

Comments: EyeSaw is a graphic design exhibition organised by the Australian Graphic Design Association (AGDA) and Sydney Design '08. It takes place in various outdoor locations throughout the city. Key objectives are to enable the public to engage with and discuss design; promote an understanding of what graphic design is to so many people as possible; broaden the promotion of graphic design in Australia. The brief was to create a smile in the mind whilst increasing the general public's awareness and recognition of graphic design. Our approach was to create a series of posters that play on some of the key traits associated with design: An eye for detail; an eye for colour; an eye for composition; an eye for beauty.

97 Post-war plastics | Design Firm: NB Studio | Creative Directors: Ben Stott, Alan Dye, Nick Finney | Designer: Daniel Lock | Client: Vitsoe

Comments: To coincide with the Victoria and Albert Museum's exhibition Cold War Modern: Design 1945~1970, international modern furniture company, Vitsoe is exhibiting the pioneering plastic furniture of its legendary German designer, Dieter Rams. NB Studio were commissioned to create the invitation and limited edition poster for the event. To create a sense of time and context, the plastic backed 601 chair was juxtaposed with an obscure 60's illustration to highlight the forward looking nature of Rams's designs. A deliberately lo-fi approach was taken to the print specification with use of an off-white paper stock to give a 60's look and feel.

98 Poster, Faculty Tour, Düsseldorf University of Applied Sciences | Design Firm: Buero Uebele Visuelle Kommunikation | Designer: Andreas Uebele, Tristan Schmitz | Printer: Karl-Heinz Janke | Client: University of Applied Sciences Düsseldorf

Comments: A tour to turn your world upside down? or a yellow ring that forges a link between architecture and communications design? the ragged type forms a safety net for this typographical balancing act.

99 Inward Gazes: Documentaries of Chinese Performance Art 2008 | Design Firm: Macao Museum of Art | Designer, Illustrator, Typographer: Chao Sioleong | Client: Chao Sioleong

100 LIFE LINE | Design Firm: Toyotsugu Itoh Design Office | Art Director, Copywriter, Designer, Illustrator, Typographer: Toyotsugu Itoh | Client: Chubu Creators Club

101 2009 Symphony Showhouse | Design Firm: Jay Advertising | Account Director: Heather Rohr | Art Director, Associate Creative Director, Illustator: Joseph Mayernik | Chief Creative Officer: Ferinand J. Smith | Copywriter: Matt Conn | Creative Director: Bob Nisson | Print Producer: Marianne Warfle | Printer: City Blue | Client: Rochester Philiharmonic Orchestra

Comment: A series of posters designed to commemorate the 2008 Rochester Philharmonic Orchestra (RPO) Symphony Showhouse. A series of custom illustrations were created to reflect unique characteristics of the Ellwanger Estate, a Rochester 19th century home.

102 100 Artists' Books | Design Firm: David Mellen Design | Designer: David Mellen | Printer: Colortek | Client: USC Doheny Library

103 Helvetica, 50 Years | Design Firm: Melchior Imboden | Designer: Melchior Imboden | Production Company: Boesch Siebdruck Ag Stans | Client: Poster-Competition for the Celebration of »Helvetica, 50 Years«

Comments: An initiative by Lars Müller in collaboration with the Museum of Design Zürich.

Fashion

104-107 Platinum PLEATS PLEASE "SUSHI" | Design Firm: Taki Satoh Design Office Inc. | Art Director: Taku Satoh | Designers: Taku Satoh, Teppei Yuyama | Photographer: Yasuaki Yoshinaga | Client: ISSEY MIYAKE INC.

108, 109 FRANCK MULLER POSTER | Design Firm: odmr design agency | Art Director: Osamu Misawa | Designer: Satomi Kajitani | Client: WORLD COMMERCE CORPORATION

Festivals

110 Park City Jazz Festival 2008 | Design Firm: Michael Schwab Studio | Art Director: Kris Severson | Designer, Illustrator: Michael Schwab | Printer: Rush Creek Editions | Client: Park City Jazz Foundation

111, 112 Platinum Sing For Gough | Design Firm: Eric Chan Design Co. Ltd. | Art Directors, Designers: Eric Chan, Iris Yu | Creative Director, Design Director: Eric Chan | Photographer: Tim Lau | Client: Gough Street Festival

Comments: This is a poster series for the Gough Festival Hong Kong. I was one of 10 designers who exhibited at Gough Street. Located between Central and Sheung Wan, Gough Street is one of the oldest streets in Hong Kong. Occupied mostly by buildings several stories high built in the 1950s and 60s,

I used the idea of residents hanging out their washing on bamboo sticks. This is described as the multi-national flags scene. Hong Kong people in the past used to hang their clothes outside the windows and the scene resembled an interesting picture of a number of national flags flying in the sky. Riding on this interesting and unique scene, the designer makes use of this common practice to form the Chinese name of Gough Street in order to remind the collective memory of audience. The red and blue cloth flying in the sky also echoes with the joyful mood of the Gough Festival.

113 2004 TEXAS BOOK FESTIVAL POSTER | Design Firm: Sibley/Peteet Design | Creative Director: Rex Peteet | Designer: Kris Worley | Illstrator: Julia Speed | Printer: Horizon Printing | Client: Texas Book Festival

Comments: Each year the Texas Book Festival chooses a Texas artist's work to use for the Festival poster. However, because the title on the poster is sometimes used without the art, the title treatment needs to be interesting enough to stand on its own. To liven up the chosen image, the line, "Ignite Your Imagination" was used along with beaming rays and a fitting type-treatment.

114 Forfattersleppet | Design Firm: Cucumber | Account Director, Art Director, Artist, Associate Creative Director, Chief Creative Officer, Creative Director, Creative Strategist, Design Director, Designer, Executive Creative DIrector, Illustrator, Project Manager, Typographer: Tonnes H Gundersen | Copywriter: Pia Ibsen | Print Producer, Production Company: Molvik Grafisk AS | Printer: Knut Molvik | Client: Norsk Forfattersentrum Vestlandet

Comments: The postert is part of a pomotional package which also comprises a brochure, adverts and big posters. The book and umbrella symbolizes literature in the rainy city Bergen.

115 Het Heiner Goebbels Festival | Design Firm: Thonik | Art Director: Joel Arbez | Copywriter: Sebastien Wilcox | Creative Director: Joe Hospodarec | Photographer: Justen Lacoursiere | Client: Het Koninklijk Conservatorium Den Haag

116, 117 5 Days of Fun | Design Firm: WAX | Art Director: Joel Arbez | Copywriter: Sebastien Wilcox | Creative Director: Joe Hospodarec | Photographer: Justen Lacoursiere | Client: Calgary International Children's Festival

118, 119 Design Firm: VSA Partners, Inc | Designer, Executive Creative Director: Dana Arnett | Client: Alliance Graphique Internacional

120 Lake Geneva Wine Festival 2008 | Design Firm: Optima Soulsight USA | Artist, Creative Director: Adam Ferguson | Client: Lake Geneva Wine Festival

Comments: Optima Soulsight developed the poster pro bono. Posters were used to promote the wine festival and were also used as a fundraising tool. Signed and numbered posters were raffled at festival events and posters are also available to purchase on the Lake Geneva Wine Festival web site. Proceeds go to local non profit organizations; Geneva Lakes YMCA, George Williams College of Aurora University, and Holiday Home Camp.

121 Hardly Strictly Bluegrass 8 | Design Firm: Goodby, Silverstein & Partners | Art Director, Photographer: Claude Shade | Executive Creative Director: Jeffery Goodby | Client: Hardly Strictly Bluegrass

122, 123 New - Russian/New | Design Firm: WONGDOODY | Art Director: Tony Zimney | Copywriter: Jennie Moore | Creative Director: Tracy Wong | Print Producer: Ken King | Client: Seattle International Film Festival

Film

124 WHITE LIGHT, BLACK RAIN | Design Firm: Kimura Design Office, Inc. | Art Director, Artist, Designer, Typographer: Yuji Kimura | Client: IWANAMI HALL

Comments: A Steven Okazaki's documentary film enlightened me. I was deep impressed with his thinking of war(especially Hiroshima and Nagasaki) and his activity. I designed the poster for sale. I contributed profit to his activity.

125 World Wide Wayne | Design Firm: One Hundred Church Street | Art Director, Designer, Illustrator: R.P. Bissland | Copywriter: Matt Basso | Printer: Lorraine Press | Project Managers: Matt Basso, Eric Blackburn | Client: American West Center

126 Wanted Teaser Poster | Design Firm: Cold Open | Agency Producer: Cold Open | Art Director: Don Pace | Chief Creative Officer: John Peed | Creative Director: Gardner DeFranceaux | Photographer: Frank Ockenfels | Production Company: Universal Pictures | Client: Frank Chiocchi

127 Doomsday Poster | Design Firm: Cold Open | Agency Producer: Cold Open | Art Director: John Peed | Chief Creative Officer: John Peed | Creative Director: Gardner DeFranceaux | Production Company: Universal Pictures | Client: Scott Abraham

128 Blindness Character Banners | Design Firm: bpg | Account Director, Creative Director: Steph Sebbag | Art Director: Steven Yi | Client: Alliance Films

129 "It Sticks with You" | Design Firm: tba advertising | Account Director: Jennifer Collins | Art Director: Audelino Moreno | Associate Creative Director: David Jenkins | Chief Creative Director: Paul Evers | Copywriter: Frank Gjata | Phtographer: Steve Tague | Print Producer: Alice LeBlond | Printer: Ryder Graphics | Client: BendFilm

130 Garbage Warrior | Design Firm: Mark Gowing Design | Art Director, Creative Director, Designer, Photographer, Typographer: Mark Gowing | Printer: Mr Copy | Copywriter: Sandie Don | Client: Hopscotch Films

Comments: Garbage Warrior is a documentary film about the architect, Michael Reynolds, who builds houses out of waste products such as bottles, cans and tyres.

131 Photographer | Design Firm: Big V Pictures | Copywriter, Creative Director: Les Merson | Designer: Beata Stolarska | Photographer: Ken Villeneuve | Printer: Horseshoe Press | Production Company: Moving Pictures | Client: Ken Villeneuve

Comments: To promote the film "Something to eat, a place to sleep & someone who gives a damn." A film about homelessness.

Food&Beverage

132 Cannonball Wine Company Poster | Design Firm: Michael Schwab Studio | Art Director: Greg Ahn | Designer, Illustrator: Michael Schwab | Client: Cannonball Wine Company

133 O's CAMPUS CAFE GRAND OPENING POSTER | Design Firm: Sibley/Peteet Design | Creative Director, Designer, Illustrator: Rex Peteet | Client: O's Campus Cafe

Comments: O's was opening in the main building on the University of Texas at Austin campus as a health food oriented cafe for folks to eat at in a contemporary settings. In conjunction with the identity, we also developed this poster to be output very large and hung up for the grand opening.

134 Grow What You Eat | Design Firm: Saint Hieronymus Press | Art Director, Artist, Designer, Printer: David Lance Goines | Client: Chez Panisse Cafe & Restaurant

135 Species | Design Firm: KreativeDept | Account Director: Kenny Sink | Art Director, Copywriter, Creative Director, Designer: Kenny Sink | Client: Studley Store

Comments: These were used in-store to remind customers that Studley Store sold only fresh meats in grocery section as well as their prepared foods section.

Lectures

136 USC School of Architecture Fall 2008 Lecture Series | Design Firm: David Whitcraft | Designer: David Whitcraft | Printer: Chromatic | Client: USC School of Architecture

Comments: I created a schedule for the lecture series at USC school of architecture that would intrigue and create interest in the events. I added two levels of information to the poster beyond the schedule and created separate grids and colors for each level. Each level became its own poster along with a composite poster. I added a layer that included a visual manifesto of my design process of the poster and an info graphic analyzing the meteorological probabilities during the time period of the events. The students and faculties covered their studios and walls with arrangements of the posters.

137 Helfand+Drenttel Lecture | Design Firm: Piscatello Design Centre | Art Director, Designer, Typographer: Rocco Piscatello | Client: Fashion Institute of Technology

Comments: Poster for the lecture given by Jessica Helfand and William Drenttel at the Fashion Institute of Technology in November 2008

Museums

138 Linnaeus Exhibition Posters | Design Firm: Naughtyfish design | Creative Director, Design Director, Designer: Paul Garbett | Client: The Macleay Museum, University of New South Wales

Comments: These posters were created to promote an exhibition celebrating the life and work of the Swedish scientist Carl von Linné.

139 Erasmus in beeld | Design Firm: Thonik | Account Director, Art Director, Designer, Typographer: Thonik | Client: Museum Boijmans van Beuningen

Comments: Identity for Museum Boijmans Van Beuningen in Rotterdam. This museum houses a collection of approximately 125,000 objects including works of old masters, modern and contemporary art and design and decorative arts. The new director Sjarel Ex wishes both to strengthen the museum's links with the city of Rotterdam and increase the museum's national and international standing. Thonik applied three processes that are at the basis of the house style for Museum Boijmans Van Beuningen. In the first place Thonik realised a shift from reduction towards complexity in the graphic variables and their rules of application. The second process involves the construction of the typeface from lines of various colours. The third process concerns the relationship between the museum's logo and the typography for its exhibitions and activities. The museum's name has been reduced to a simple, stable and modest logotype while the typography for the posters and invitations is the bearer of the museum's identity. The museum's identity has shifted from the name of the sender towards the form and content of its activities. Museum Boijmans Van Beuningen's house style applies a marketing technique—branding—but the way it is implemented within a flexible typographic system contrasts strongly with the formal language that prevails in commercial branding. In its innovative and experimental character, the graphic system developed by Thonik connects with the productions branded by it: art in the broad sense of the word. The house style is applied consistently across all the museum's means of communications: on exhibition announcements, in the museum's wayfinding system, in merchandising, advertising and on the website. The new house style for Museum Boijmans Van Beuningen fits the museum self image and its ambition as a 'performing institute': its identity is formed by the totality of its achievements.

140 Soakers | Design Firm: Thonik | Account Director: Thonik | Art Director, Creative Director, Designer, Typographer: Thonik | Client: Museum Boijmans van Beuningen

Comments: Same as page 139.

141 Tony Labat/SFMOMA I Want You Call for Entries Poster | Design Firm: San Francisco Museum of Modern Art | Art Director: Jennifer Sonderby | Designers: Jeremy Mende, Jennifer Bagheri | Printer: PS Printsmart | Client: San Francisco Museum of Modern Art

Comments: Working closely with the artist, this poster was designed to announce an interdisciplinary and multi-part project designed by Tony Labat, that draws on historical propaganda, electoral systems, and American Idol. I Want You invites audiences to make their own popular demands audible in a variety of forms: slogan, public performance, city-wide poster, and artist video.

142 Design MMoCA | Design Firm: Hiebing | Art Director, Designer: Barry Kalpinski | Copywriter: Sandy Geier | Creative Director: Peter Bell | Print Producer: Chris Richard | Project Manager: Sam Ganebom | Client: Madison Museum of Contemporary Art

Comments: The Madison Museum of Contemporary Art asked Hiebing to help publicize a first of its kind exhibit "Design MMoCA" for which interior designers were invited to create living spaces around art from the museum's permanent collection. The result was a series of printed pieces using color, patterns and texture to create illustrations representing key elements of interior design. In a nod to the exhibit's concept, the illustrations contain the letterform "M" from MMoCA.

Credits&Comments

143, 144 Maze Posters | Design Firm: 3 Advertising | Account Director: Chris Moore | Art Director, Designer: Tim McGrath | Copywriter, Creative Director: Sam Maclay | Client: The National Museum of Nuclear Science & History

Comments: This series of posters for the National Museum of Nuclear Science & History communicates the client's goal of inviting reaction and thoughtful debate about the use of nuclear technology. The posters convey an open invitation for people of all political beliefs and persuasions to experience the museum.

145 minimumaximumuseum | Design Firm: STUDIO INTERNATIONAL | Agency Producer: STUDIO INTERNATIONAL | Account Director, Art Director, Artist, Associate Creative Director, Chief Creative Officer, Copywriter, Creative Director, Creative Strategist, Design Director, Designer, Executive Creative Director, Illustrator, Photographer, Typographer: Boris Ljubicic | Production Company: STUDIO INTERNATIONAL | Project Manager: Visnja Zgaga, MDC | Client: MDC-Museum Documentation Centre

Comments: A poster for International Museum Day emphasizes the enlightenment function of the museum institution. By merging the words minimum/maximum/museum into an unbroken string, the information has been converted to an ornament which, under lamp light, is revealed as text in the centre of the poster. In museum minimum and maximum are made of exhibits and exhibition, and very oftenly minimum becomes maximum and maximum becomes minimum. That is why are the words minimum maximum museum connected in one word :minimumaximumuseum !

146 The New Wing Luke Asian Museum | Design Firm: WONGDOODY | Account Directors: Susan Hayden, Mark Sloane | Copywriter: George Mollas | Creative Director: Tan Le | Designer: Dave Goedde | Digital Artist/Multimedia: Claire Knue, Charlie Rakatansky | Print Producer: Stacy McCann | Client: Wing Luke Asian Museum

147 Secession | Design Firm: KMS TEAM | Account Director: Sandra Ehm | Creative Director: Knut Maierhofer | Design Director: Patrick Märki | Designer: Bettina Otto | Client: Villa Stuck

Comments: The Munich Secession was a group of artists which was formed in 1892 to break away from the conventional academic mainstream of the time, based on the example of Paris; its members included Franz von Stuck, Lovis Corinth and Max Liebermann. For the retrospective at Villa Stuck we designed a poster based solely on typography: the word "secession" appears divided into three blocks of three letters each; the font selected was Gill, not only because it is the signature font used by Villa Stuck but also because it provides a formal match with the art nouveau lettering of the logo and thus implicitly refers to the relevant turn-of-the-century period. By doing without a pictorial motif, it was also possible to adopt a neutral position in relation to the plurality of styles of the various artists represented within the Secession. With its stringent reduction (no colours or pictures, and an ample white space which provides a formally "positive" logo), the poster stood out especially well among the colourful diversity of cultural advertising which was especially intensive during the Munich's 850th anniversary celebrations.

Music

148 Black Crowes | Design Firm: The Martin Agency | Art Director: Mark Brye | Creative Director: Mike Hughes | Client: National Theatre

149 Fillmore Jazz Festival | Design Firm: Saint Hieronymus Press | Art Director, Artist, Designer, Illustrator, Typographer, Printer: David Lance Goines | Client: Fillmore Jazz Festival

150 Platinum latespot | Design Firm: gggrafik-design | Art Director, Artist, Creative Director, Designer, Typographer: Goetz Gramlich | Print Producer, Printer: Gerscher Siebdruck | Production Company: gggrafik | Client: jazz festival willisau

Comments: The LateSpot, a small party location on the Jazz Festival Willisau, only opens late in the night. So i choosed nightglowing colors to promote the club, glowing strong and long in a different color than the daylightcolor.

151 Duke Ellington Concert | Design Firm: One Hundred Church Street | Art Director, Designer, Illustrator: R.P. Bissland | Printer: FedEx Kinkos | Client: Jazz Kicks Band

Comments: Designed to announce a Jazz Concert of an evening of Duke Ellington music as performed by the Jazz Kicks Band, a local band made up of professionals lead by the master jazz musician, Larry Smith. Its intended audience is the general public and is posted at various locations around Northern Utah. It is meant to compete with the many other posted events vying for the attention of the college town audience.

152 Chris Vadala Concert | Design Firm: One Hundred Church Street | Designer, Illustrator: R.P. Bissland | Printer: FedEx Kinkos | Project Manager: Jon Gudmonson | Client: Department of Music, Utah State University

Comments: Each year the Department of Music at Utah State University puts on an annual jazz concert with a nationally known jazz musician. The chosen musician puts on a concert for the general public where she or he gives a solo performance and also accompanies the Utah State Jazz Band. The musician also gives seminars, coordinates jam sessions and teaches workshops with, and for, students in the jazz program. This poster was designed to promote the Chris Vadala concert. Mr. Vadala, this year's jazz musician, is an accomplished and popular solo performer. He is also one of the founding members of and still performs with the Chuck Mangione Quartet. Mr. Vadala is known as the "Woodwind Guru" for his ability to play any woodwind instrument with unusually gifted artistry. The poster is posted at various locations in and around Northern Utah.

153 Annual Festival Concert Poster | Design Firm: Paone Design Associates | Art Director, Typographer: Gregory Paone | Designers, Photographers: Gregory Paone, Joshua Bankes | Printer: Fidelity Graphics | Client: Philadelphia Youth Orchestra

Comments: The Philadelphia Youth Orchestra commissioned Paone Design Associates to produce its Annual Festival Concert Posters. This year, PYO's program included the world premiere "Concerto for Bass Trombone and Orchestra", which provided inspiration for the poster artwork. In addition to the photography, PDA also created the orchestra's proprietary typeface which is utilized as a display font in the posters and program books.

154 13 Ghosts Poster | Design Firm: Joel Wheat Designs | Artist, Designer: Joel Wheat | Client: Bottletree

155 Kvartetit ritarihuoneella | Design Firm: Original Loiri Oy | Art Director, Designer: Pekka Loiri | Printer: Nykypaino Oy | Client: New Helsinki Quartett

Comments: Poster for a consert serie Kvartetit ritarihuoneella/ String Quartetos in The Helsinki Noble House

156 Jazz Ltd. | Design Firm: john rieben design | Designer: John Rieben | Typographer: John Rieben | Client: Kewaunee Inn

Comments: Announce a weekend jazz event to be held in the newly opened Hammachec Cultural facility along Lake Michigan's northern shore.

157 Built to Spill | Design Firm: The Martin Agency | Art Director: Adam Stockton | Creative Director: Mike Hughes | Client: National Theatre

158 Untitled | Design Firm: Self Employed | Art Director: Jeroen van Erp | Designer: Chris van Diemen | Printer: Yeehaa Print, Scotland | Typographer: Chris van Diemen | Client: The Blue Nile

Comments: Poster Design for a few shows of the legendary The Bue Nile playing at The Royal Concert Hall in Glasgow, Scotland. Printed (offset) in two colours (black and silver metallic), not only seen on the streets in Glsgow in A3-format, but the poster was also (screen)printed on a much bigger size: 40inch by 60inch.

159 Poster for new album "in the whale" | Design Firm: hitman corporation | Art Director, Designer: Atsushi Yamada | Photographer: Sadato Ishizuka | Photographer's Assistant: Shinpo Kimura | Client: Metro-Ongen

Comments: Promotion for Japanese post-rock band Metro-Onegen's new album "in the whale". This image was also used in CD cover. The title means our world is stalled with no way out, especially in Japan. I express the situation with this image. I didn't use photo retouching in this image. I took this image by putting ices on the photo which was print outed.

160 Mark Helias & Open Loose | Design Firm: Niklaus Troxler Design | Art Director, Designer, Typographer: Niklaus Troxler | Printer: Boesch Silkscreen Stans | Client: Jazz in Willisau

Comments: Poster for a Jazz concert with the group "Mark Helias & Open Loose". I printed the black and white typography on existing posters. So each one looked different, but all the information was readable, because the black and white color had enough contrast over the pre-printed posters.

161 Der Rote Bereich (The Red Area) | Design Firm: Niklaus Troxler Design | Art Director, Designer, Typographer: Niklaus Troxler | Client: Jazz in Willisau

Comments: Poster for a Jazz Group with name "The Red Area".

Opera

162, 163, 164 Design Firm: GEISSBUEHLER | Designer: GEISSBUEHLER | Client: opermhaus zürich

165 The Tales of Hoffmann Poster | Design Firm: TOKY BRANDING+DESIGN | Creative Director: Eric Thoelke | Designer: Travis Brown | Digital Artist/Multimedia: Adam Fischer | Client: Opera Theatre Saint Louis

Comments: In the opera,"The Tales of Hoffmann," a drunken man recollects dreams of three women—a mechanical doll, a bejeweled siren, and the daughter of a famous composer—all of whom break his heart. The poster was used as a limited edition fine art poster for the OTSL patrons.

Photographers

166 Beach Blanket | Design Firm: Chris Sanders | Creative Directors: Giovanni Russo, Patrick Casey | Client: Chris Sanders

Comments: Poster Created for Self Promotion of Chris Sanders Photography. Sent to 6000 Clients Worldwide.

167 Void / Shufti Magazine Volume 6 | Design Firm: Sean Kennedy Santos fotografie | Account Director, Agency Producer: Gabrielle Fitzgerald | Art Director, Artist, Associate Creative Director, Copywriter, Creative Director, Photographer: Sean Kennedy Santos | Design Director, Special Process: Jon Banks | Designer: Vast agency, London | Executive Creative Directors: Matt Austin, Jon Banks | Printer: GF Smith, London | Production Company: Vast agency | Project Manager, Typographer: Phil Morrison | Client: Sean Kennedy Santos

Comments: To promote special edition of the 6th volume of the fashion publication ' Shufti Mag ' that incorporates the best of design and single photographer / storyline .The poster is used to extend awareness during it's release, in galleries and design retail stores throughout New York and London. Aimed at the new designers and fashion based clients who use design and photography as a form of advertising product in a book / publishing content .

Political

168 Diplomacy | Designer, Illustrator: Jason Dietrick | Client: Power to the Poster.org

169 Drums of war | Design Firm: Texas State University-San Marcos | Art Director, Designers: Jeffrey Davis, Claudia Röschmann | Associate Creative Director: Claudia Röschmann | Creative Director: William Meek | Illustrator: Jeffrey Davis | Project Managers: William Meek, Claudia Röschmann | Client: www.globalpeacenow.com

Comments: There is a price to pay for oil that is greater than the price paid at the pump. That price is peace—the first casualty of war. Most Americans have forgotten this and that the Iraq war is about oil and will always be about oil!

170 DeFence? | Design Firm: Studio Joseph Jibri | Account Director, Art Director, Associate Creative Director, Chief Creative Officer, Copywriter, Creative Director, Creative Strategist, Design Director, Designer, Executive Creative Director, Executive Creative Strategist, Photographer, Print Producer, Project Manager, Typographer: Joseph Jibri | Printer: Kal Press Ltd. | Agency Producer, Production Company: Studio Joseph Jibri | Client: Joseph Jibri self project

Comments: Israel 58 years of independence reflected in a poster dealing with the fence/wall under construction.

171 Before/After | Design Firm: Scorsone/Drueding: SDPOSTERS.COM | Art Director, Designer: Joe Scorsone, Alice Drueding | Client: Good Design Cultural Association, Milan

172 Homeland Security | Design Firm: Scorsone/Drueding: SDPOSTERS.COM | Art Directors, Designers: Joe Scorsone, Alice Drueding | Client: SDPOSTERS.COM

Comments: This poster addresses the way we are imprisoned by our fear of terrorism when we allow action against terrorism to result in the loss of personal freedoms.

173 Requiem | Design Firm: Studio Uwe Loesch | Art Director, Copywriter, Designer: Uwe Loesch | Photographer: Jochen Moll, 1957 | Printer: Color Druck Essen | Client: G8 Hokkaido Toyaka Summit 2008

174 Made In China | Design Firm: Zc Creative | Designer: Scott Laserow | Client: Secretariat of Sichuan China

175 White Obama | Design Firm: WONGDOODY | Art Director, Creative Director: Tracy Wong | Copywriters: Martin Luther King Jr., John Schofield, Tony Ober | Digital Artist/Multimedia: Charlie Rakatansky | Client: Citizen 2023

176 Vote For Me | Design Firm: EMdash Design | Art Director, Creative Director, Designer, Photographer: Elizabeth Maplesden | Copywriters: Elizabeth Maplesden (top of poster), AIGA Design for Democracy (bottom bar) | Client: AIGA Design for Democracy

Comments: This poster was part of the AIGA's 2008 Get Out the Vote effort. As stated in the rules for this project, the message should be nonoffensive and nonpartisan. The intent of this poster is to impress upon eligible but apathetic voters the importance of voting in the upcoming election. Vote For Me, targeted to those who consider voting a difficult task, shows the possible consequence of not voting: inadvertently electing a tyrant (in the form of the wolf politician) into office.

Tyranny doesn't make excuses, so why should voters make excuses about not voting? By not paying attention to the election, the non-voter is allowing one of the most obviously bad candidates to win. At the time the poster was designed (April 2008), the political field had not been finalized. The poster was published on the AIGA's Get Out the Vote section. A downloadable PDF is available from this site as well.

177 Collateral Damage | Design Firm: Ryan Russell Design | Art Director, Designer, Photographer: Ryan Russell | Client: Good 50x70

Comments: This was done as an option for the Good 50x70 poster project.

178 Rhetoric | Design Firm: Hyperakt Design Group | Artist, Designer: Deroy Peraza | Project Manager: Rosemary Hahn | Client: Hyperakt

Comments: Placing quotes from Barack Obama's various public speeches in bright, neon lettering against a black background, further meaning can be deciphered by highlighting key words of the text, revealing the core truths behind Obama's messages of hope.

179 History | Design Firm: Hyperakt Design Group | Artist, Designer: Deroy Peraza | Printer: Clone Press | Project Manager: Rosemary Hahn | Client: Hyperakt

Comments: In the spirit of the powerful artwork created by political propaganda posters of the past, Obama's historic run for the American presidency is memorialized in this set of posters in varying colors; with only the word 'History' set against his iconically recognizable face.

180 "Bushed" Poster | Design Firm: Pirtle Design Inc. | Art Director, Illustrator: Woody Pirtle | Designer: Scarlet Duba | Client: 30 reasons.org

Printers

181 Heidelberg demonstration posters | Design Firm: Counterpart Communication Design | Account Director: Elizabeth Brown | Art Director, Designer: Sara Backus | Copywriter: Sheperd Simmons | Printer: Imec | Client: Imec

Comments: A series of small 9 x 16 inch posters printed on Imec's new Heidelberg press, and sent to area production managers, as a demonstration of it's capabilities. Printed four color process, plus spot metallic silver, spot gloss varnish and spot dull varnish.

Products

182 Revolution Poster | Design Firm: Staccato | Account Director: Sara Elizalde | Art Director: Arvin Mendoza | Creative Director: Stacy Butchart | Illustrator: Jeff Foster | Print Producer: Nick Dechenne | Client: Biamp Systems

183 STEP STEP of Motomi Kawakami Design | Design Firm: Shin Matsunaga Design Inc. | Art Director: Shin Matsunaga | Designers: Shin Matsunaga, Moemi Kiyokawa | Client: KAWAKAMI DESIGN ROOM

184 Spore | Design Firm: Rose Design | Designer: Simon Elliott | Photographer: Tom Mannion | Printer: Push | Client: Jinny Blom Limited

Comments: When multi-award winning landscape designer Jinny Blom asked us to help launch her new furniture range—Spore—we had a pretty good idea we wouldn't end up photographing them in a studio. The handmade stools are inspired by the definition of spores: 'reproductive structures which can adapt for easy dispersion in natural environments'. Which is why the image, typography, and choice of paper, looks and feels the way it does.

185, 186 AquaMarkLX Posters | Design Firm: Marriner Marketing | Account Directors: Susan Gunther, Mike Deming | Art Director: Daniel Vong | Copywriter: Jeff Grutkowski | Creative Director: Bill Mitchell | Illustrator: Paula Airesman | Print Producer: Dave Wolinski | Client: ARAMARK

Comments: This poster series, designed for an internal sales promotion for AquaMark pure water dispensers, motivates and inspires sales people by positioning them as office heroes. The posters remind the sales people that to make a dramatic, positive impact on their clients' workplaces, all they have to do is "Just add water" with an AquaMarkLX pure water dispenser.

187 Bell Canoe Campaign | Design Firm: Carmichael Lynch | Art Director, Illustrator: Doug Pedersen | Copywriter: Heath Pochucha | Creative Director: Mike Haeg | Executive Creative Director: Jim Nelson | Print Producers: Ember Kapitan, Linda Hines | Client: Bell Canoe

ProfessionalServices

188 100% | Design Firm: Grabarz & Partner Werbeagentur GmbH | Art Directors: Tomas Tulinius, Katharina Wlodasch, Florian Pack | Chief Creative Officer, Creative Director: Ralf Heuel | Copywriters: Bent Hartmann, Teja Fischer, Gerrit Steffen | Photographers: Julia Christe c/o Kombinatrotweiss, Nico Weymann, Tom Grammerstorf c/o Birgit Stöver | Client: Farbraum Digital Art GmbH

189, 190 Art Serving Capitalism | Design Firm: Goodby, Silverstein & Partners | Designer: Brian Gunderson, Erin Dahlbeck | Executive Creative Directors: Jeffrey Goodby, Rich Silverstein | Client: Goodby, Silverstein & Partners

191 Local Knowledge | Design Firm: The Partners | Copywriter: Nick Asbury | Creative Director: Jack Renwick | Designers: Tim Brown, Tim Fishlock | Executive Creative Strategist: Martin Rowlett | Project Manager: Hannah Weir | Artworker: Simon Cranwell | Client: Wolf Theiss

Comments: As part of their new identity, leading Eastern European law firm Wolf Theiss sent a large format posters to all their offices. Displayed in reception areas, these posters are a reminder of their significant growth over the years and their unrivalled local knowledge across the region. Map pins mark the office locations.

Public&SocialServices

192, 193 madworld | Design Firm: mad studios | Art Director, Copywriter, Creative Director, Designer: brian LAU | Photographer: zeroc HON | Client: JIUU group of creatives

Comments: This is a series of posters intended to arouse awareness and reflection of the overly materialistic society that hong kong has become, the dangers of such a society and the need for moderation.

194 Flag | Design Firm: The Martin Agency | Art Director, Designer: Jamie Mahoney | Copywriter: John Mahoney | Creative Directors: Sean Riley, Danny Robinson | Client: WE

195 Love Yourself | Design Firm: taber calderon | Art Director, Artist, Copywriter, Designer, Typographer: Taber Calderon | Client: Good 50x70

196 Use Your Head–Wear a Condom! | Design Firm: Scorsone/Drueding: SDPOSTERS.COM | Art Directors, Copywriters, Designers, Illustrators: Joe Scorsone, Alice Drueding | Client: Good Design Cultural Association, Milan

Comments: This poster was designed to remind viewers in a humorous way about the importance of safe sexual practices. The client, Good Design Cultural Association, made this poster available to international health organizations around the world.

197 MR | Design Firm: CURIOUS | Creative Director: Peter Rae | Designer, Illustrator: Matt Davies | Client: CURIOUS

Comments: As part of a special issue on tackling gang culture in the UK, the Independent on Sunday in the UK asked CURIOUS to create a hard-hitting poster campaign. Ours was featured prominently—an image of a child's profile merged with a handgun, to alert parents to think about what their kids are up to.

198 Shark Man Poster | Design Firm: Brogan & Partners | Agency Producer: Chris Stamper | Account Director: Julie Hayworth-Perman | Art Director: Vong Lee | Copywriter: Gabe Cherry | Creative Director: Laurie Hix | Executive Creative Director: Bonnie Folster | Client: Center for Responsible Lending

Comments: This is a transit poster designed to motivate people to get involved in the campaign to stop predatory lending. It was targeted at decision makers in Washington DC.

199 Storm Drain Campaign | Design Firm: DDB Los Angeles | Account Director: Debbie Rodriguez | Agency Producer: Paul Newman | Art Director: Kevin McCarthy | Artists: Blob Steve Vance, Thing Owen Richardson, Zombie Dave McMacken | Chief Creative Officer: Mark Monteiro | Copywriter: Jeff Spiegel | Creative Directors: Kevin McCarthy, Jeff Spiegel | Client: Heal The Bay

Comments:

Purpose – to raise awareness that dumping waste and chemicals into our neighborhood storm drains is dangerous, as well as being not a solution, but a source for new and bigger problems.

Solution – to use images from horror films, and humor, to get peoples' attention, and make them consider the long-term effects of their actions.

200 Bless China | Design Firm: 601bisang | Art Director, Creative Director, Illustrator: Park Kumjun | Designera: Park Kum-jun, You Na-won | Client: New Graphic Magazine

Comments: The "Bless China" poster was designed for a humanitarian aid project to help the victims of the destructive earthquake that hit China on May 12th, 2008. The Bless China message is accentuated by the inspiration taken from the oriental talisman that is believed to protect the bearer from disasters and bring good luck.

201 Dotted Line | Design Firm: The Martin Agency | Art Director, Designer, Copywriter: John Mahoney | Creative Directors: Sean Riley, Danny Robinson | Client: WE

Publishing

202-204 Age of metal collar | Design Firm: Shin Matsunaga Design Inc. | Art Director, Designer, Artist: Shin Matsunaga | Client: SHOGAKUKAN INC.

205 Another Sky | Design Firm: SVIDesign | Designer, Illustrator, Photographer, Typographer: Sasha Vidakovic | Client: Profile Books

Comments: Poster promoting the book containing writings of authors whom been imprisoned by oppressive regimes.

Retail

206 Balls | Design Firm: Grabarz & Partner Werbeagentur GmbH | Art Director: Vanessa Iff | Creative Directors: Ralf Heuel, Dirk Siebenhaar | Photographer: Christian Kerber c/o Waldmann Solar | Client: IKEA Deutschland GmbH & Co. KG

207 2008 Brand Graphic Posters | Design Firm: Fossil | Art Director: Dru McCabe | Creative Director: Stephen Zhang | Designers: Dustin Wallace, Rachel Voglewede, Jean Paul Khabbaz, Brent Couchman | Client: Fossil

Credits&Comments

208 Defend Your Base | Design Firm: Howard, Merrell & Partners | Agency Producer: Ann Neely | Art Director: John Moore | Copywriter: Steve Olshansky | Creative Director: Billy Barnes | Photographer: Gary Land | Print Producer: Robin Rogers | Project Manager: Stephanie Dunford | Client: Cordura

Comments: Cordura Baselayer fabric was designed specifically for combat soldiers. As in, they're going to wear this stuff while they're over the wire and their lives are on the line. We had to be cool. We had to be authentic. We had to be use military intelligence. Mission accomplished. These posters were done to create awareness and intrigue in-store and at special military events.

209, 210 Queen Victoria's Makeover | Design Firm: Frost Design | Copywriter: Nigel Malone | Creative Director: Vince Frost | Design Director: Anthony Donovan | Designer: Adrian Hing | Project Manager: Beverley Hall | Client: IPOH - Queen Victoria Buildings

Comments: In 2008 Sydney's prestigious Queen Victoria Building commenced a refurbishment programme to enhance its' heritage value and appeal as a world-class shopping destination. A two-year project, including a new Victorian-inspired colour scheme more reflective of the original, QVB's management wanted to ensure valued customers and visitors were informed of the refurbishment and suffered no inconvenience. In response to this brief, we devised a series of in-house and street posters that drew attention to the QVB's makeover, by drawing on the key positioning of 'fashion palace' and the simple message of "let the refurbishments begin, let the shopping continue".

211 Problem & Solution | Design Firm: Carmichael Lynch | Art Director: Brad Harrison | Copywriter: Ellie Anderson | Creative Director: Sheldon Clay | Executive Creative Director: Jim Nelson | Client: Sailor's World Marina & Boat Club

Sports

212 Leaks | Design Firm: Lindsay, Stone & Briggs | Art Director, Associate Creative Director: Matt Johanning | Chief Creative Officer, Creative Director: Bill Winchester | Copywriter: Lee Schmidt | Illustrator: Jesse Zamjahn | Photographer: Dave Gilo | Client: Wisconsin Fencing Academy

213 Moto X | Design Firm: The Martin Agency | Art Director: Mark Brye | Copywriter: Cedric Giese | Creative Director: Rob Shapiro | Client: X Games

Comments: This poster and separate sticker were sold at the event as a set. The owner could then place the Moto X world championship logo sticker on the poster however they saw fit once the poster was hung.

214 Outhouses | Design Firm: Bailey Lauerman | Art Directors: Ron Sack, James Strange | Artist: Joe McDermott | Associate Creative Director: Raliegh Drenon | Chief Creative Officer: Carter Weitz | Photographer: Mike Klevetor | Printer: Jacob North | Print Producer: Brian Robinson | Client: Lincoln Marathon

Comments: This year's Lincoln Marathon poster features a row of vintage Civil War outhouses. The premise: To combine the visual language of the 1800s with the ubiquitous symbol of modern marathons—the seemingly endless row of port-a-potties.

215 Boonen Tattoo | Design Firm: Goodby, Silverstein & Partners | Art Director: Wyeth Koppenhavers | Associate Creative Director: Frank Aldorf | Copywriter: Nick Prout | Executive Creative Director: Rich Silverstein | Illustrator: Royal Post Club (CGI) | Photographer: Jens Boldt | Print Producer: Renata Robinson | Client: Specialized

Theater

216 "A Doll's House" Poster | Design Firm: co:lab | Art Director, Copywriter, Designer, Typographer: co:lab | Photographer: Derek Dudek | Printer: Thames Printing Company | Client: Bated Breath Theatre Company

Comments: Promotional poster for Bated Breath Theatre company's new take on "A Doll's House". This fresh and contemporary rewrite focused on the tension and struggle for power between husband and wife. The design aimed at highlighting this dynamic / turbulent relationship and taking this classic play out of the it's normal setting.

217 King Lear | Design Firm: WONGDOODY | Account Director: Eva Doak | Designer, Illustrator, Photographer: Ross Hogin | Client: Rough Play Productions

218 as you like | Design Firm: Original Loiri Oy | Art Director, Designer: Pekka Loiri | Printer: Indigo Print | Client: Arena

Comments: Poster for a travelling theatre Arena for a version of Shakespeares play As You like.

219 Red Death Poster | Design Firm: Curious Representation | Designer, Photographer: Joseph Coates | Client: UMBC Theatre Department

Comments: This poster for a university theatre production open to the public is made of composite images. The clouds are off my back porch this summer and shot with a 12 megapixel SLR. The statue was photographed near Berlin at Sanssoucci Palace in 1993 with 35mm black and white film. The play is a contemporary murder mystery based on the short story by Edgar Allen Poe.

220 (top left) Mutters Courage | Design Firm: Atelier Bundi | Art Director, Artist, Creative Director, Designer, Illustrator, Print Producer, Set Desginer & Props: Stephan Bundi | Printer: Serigraphie Uldry | Production Company: Theater Biel Solothurn | Project Manager: Birgit Achatz | Client: Theater Biel Solothurn

Comments: The true Story about Tabori's mother, escaped on the way to the concentration camp.

220 (top right) Boccaccio | Design Firm: Atelier Bund | Art Director, Artist, Creative Director, Designer, Photographer, Typographer: Stephan Bundi | Printer: Serigraphie Uldry | Production Company: Theater Biel Solothurn | Project Manager: Birgit Achatz | Client: Theater Biel Solothurn

Comments: A play about cuckolded (italian = horned) husbands

220 (bottom left) L' Isola Disabitata | Design Firm: Atelier Bund | Art Director, Creative Director, Designer, Photographer, Set Desginer & Props: Stephan Bundi | Printer: Serigraphie Uldry | Production Company: Theater Biel Solothurn | Project Manager: Birgit Achatz | Client: Theater Biel Solothurn

Comments: The uninhabited island (Opera by Joseph Haydn)

220 (bottom right) Romeo und Julia auf dem Dorfe | Design Firm: Atelier Bund | Creative Director, Art Director, Designer, Artist, Illustrator, Print Producer: Stephan Bundi | Printer: Serigraphie Uldry | Production Company: Theater Biel Solothurn | Project Manager: Birgit Achatz | Client: Theater Biel Solothurn

Comments: Romeo and Juliet in the village (Swiss version of Romeo and Juliet – a true story)

221 Platinum Tartuffe | Design Firm: Atelier Bundi | Account Director, Agency Producer, Artist, Creative Director, Design Director, Designer, Photographer, Typographer: Stephan Bundi | Printer: Serigraphie Uldry | Production Company: Theater Biel Solothurn | Project Manager: Birgit Achatz | Client: Theater Biel Solothurn

Comments: Tartuffe, the "false" saint.

222 Oliver Twist Play | Design Firm: Faulkner Advertising | Creative Directors: Doreen Edwards, Bob Faulkner | Account Director: Jil Gilbert | Copywriter, Typographer: Bob Faulkner | Illustrators: Bob Faulkner, Kai Faulkner | Photographer: Doreen Edwards | Printer: Western Web Printing | Production Company: Big E and Maureen | Client: Open Alternative School

Comments: Small poster for a combined 4th and 5th grade class play.

223 The Sleeper poster | Design Firm: University of Wisconsin-Green Bay | Art Director, Designer, Illustrator: Toni Damkoehler | Client: University of Wisconsin-Green Bay Theatre

Comments: I illustrated and designed the "The Sleeper" poster for the University of Wisconsin-Green Bay theatre discipline. The poster was used to inform the public of the play and to solicit an audience (to sell tickets) for that play. It was displayed in City of Green Bay area cultural centers and at the University.

224, 225 Show Posters | Design Firm: Counterform | Chief Creative Officer, Content Strategist, Creative Director, Designer, Project Manager: Kurt Saberi | Print Producer, Printer: Image Media, Portland, Oregon | Client: Artists Repertory Theatre

Comments: The Artists Repertory Theatre is Portland's oldest professional theater. For more than 20 years they have challenged artists and audiences with plays of depth and vibrancy in their two off-Broadway sized sleek and comfortable theaters. This entry is a series of 8 show posters for Artists Repertory Theater in Portland, Oregon. The posters were designed to promote the shows and increase single ticket sales.

One conceptual image for each show was developed suggesting the nature of the show content. Posters were displayed inside the lobby of the theatre and on the exterior of the building.

226 Plays for the season 2007-2008 | Design Firm: BEK Design | Art Director, Creative Director, Designer: Bulent Erkmen | Photographer: Serdar Tanyeli | Print Producer: Ofset Printhouse | Production Company: BEK Design | Client: Istanbul State Theatre

227 "About Shakespeare" | Design Firm: TeamDesign | Designer, Illustrator: Olga Sokolovskaya | Client: TeamDesign

Comments: A series of posters is an art project of TeamDesign, Moscow studio dedicated to Shakespeare. Aims to promote reading and to support «creative reading» programs and theater projects. The main theme of posters—the man is absolutely free and is not doomed.

Tourism

228 Banciao Image – Moon | Design Firm: HUGTOP Design Company | Art Director, Creative Director, Designer: Lin Horng-Jer | Client: Taiwan Poster Design Association

229 Harbor Your Dreams | Design Firm: john rieben design | Artist, Copywriter, Designer, Typographer: John Rieben | Printer, Production Company: Speedy Reprographics | Client: Kewaunee Camber of Commerce

Comments: A stylistic attempt to depict the physical attributes of the coastal village and attract visitors.

230 Mammoth "Unbound" Posters | Design Firm: Hornall Anderson | Art Director: David Bates | Creative Director: Jack Anderson | Designer: Javas Lehn | Typographer: Julie Lock | Client: Mammoth

Comments: Unbound is a series of 77 parks/runs. We recommended the Unbound experience be more radical and loose and expressive. So, we took the Mammoth logo as a post applied element like a spraypainted image and turned it upside down to be more freestyle.

A little reminiscent of a "U." The starting point was to give Unbound it's own visual system by flipping the identity upside down. Since it is a sub-culture within Mammoth, we wanted to link the two together to give the Unbound people a way to express themselves. Casual, earthy application of color of logos.

Typography

231 Go for it | Design Firm: alextrochut.com | Art Director, Typographer: Alex Trochut | Client: If you could

Comments: Extracted from www.ifyoucould.co.uk.

"Every month of 2008 If You Could will be releasing two new screenprints, one from an established artist and one from an emerging.Responding to the question, 'If you could do anything tomorrow, what would it be?', these two colour, B2 (655 x 480 mm), limited edition screenprints are only available to buy from the If You Could website for the duration of that month."

My poster is a custom modular lettering saying "go for it".

232-234 Type Faces | Design Firm: ken-tsai lee design studio | Art Directors, Designers: ken-tsai lee, Chiung-Hui Chiu | Creative Director, Copywriter: ken-tsai lee | Client: Self-promotion

235, 236 22. bundestreffen forum typografie | Design Firm: visuelle kommunikation | Designers: Tino Grass, Andreas Conradi, Martin Hoffmann, Tristan Schmitz, Andreas Uebele | Client: forum typografie e.v.

Comments: The task was to conceive and realise a corporate design for the largest typography event in Germany. At the event, acclaimed typographers delivered speeches about type design and designing type. The process of their work, from initial sketches to final typeface, was shown in an exhibition entitled "Schriftgestalten".

The corporate design to be created for the event had to follow the strict typographical rules in corporate design. The creative interpretation and application of these rules focussed on the design elements of the wordmarks and special characters.

237 HISD | Design Firm: stereo-type | Art Director, Typographer: Jaewon Seok | Client: Hongik. Viscom.

Comments: Poster for Visual communication design, Hongik University.

238 FONT: 2070 | Design Firm: Mehmet Ali Türkmen | Art Director, Illustrator, Typographer: Mehmet Ali Türkmen | Copywriter: Bilge Karasu | Client: Iyi Matbaa

Comments: Font – 2070 (Glacials that regulate our earth's climate are expected to melt completely in 2070. 'Font: 2070' it is designed for that year). And a Poster Design with the Font: 2070. A quotation from Bİ LGE Karasu's book called 'Night'.

ContributorsDirectory

3 Advertising www.whois3.com
1550 Mercantile Avenue NE, Second Floor, Albuquerque, NM 87107
United States | Tel 505 293 2333 | Fax 505 293 1198

601bisang
481-11 Seogyo-dong Mapo-gu, Seoul, 121-842, South Korea
Tel +82 2 332 2601 | Fax +82 2 332 2602

702 Design Works
3-6-6, Uehara, 1-A , Oak House, Shibuya-ku, Tokyo 151-0064, Japan
Tel +813 3468 9702 | Fax +813 3468 9797

A2/SW/HK www.a2swhk.co.uk
Unit G3, 35-42 Charlotte Road, London, EC2A 3PD, United Kingdom
Tel +44 0 20 7739 4249 | Fax +020 7739 4249

AHN kiyoung Design Room
MejyonTaihou 1206go, tomoi5-2-50, Higashi-osaka, Osaka 577-0816
Japan | Tel +81 90 9319 9396

alextrochut.com alextrochut.com
Passeig Colom, 3 Entl 3, Barcelona 08002, Spain
Tel +0034669867066 | Fax +669867066

Apre blog.livedoor.jp/tukiyo
Nagono-Heights 1F, 2-18-2, Nagono, Nishi-ku, Nagoya 451-0042
Japan | Tel +81 052 533 0971 | Fax +81 052 533 0971

Atelier Bundi www.atelierbundi.ch
Schlossstrasse 78, Boll, Berne CH-3067, Switzerland
Tel +41 31 981 00 55 | Fax +41 31 981 00 85

Bailey Lauerman www.baileylauerman.com
1248 O Street, Suite 900, Lincoln NE 68508, United States
Tel 402 479 0235

BEK Design
Tesvikiye Caddesi, 133/9 Nisantasi, Istanbul 34367, Turkey
Tel +0212 343 99 10

Big V Pictures www.bigvpictures.com
505-1763 Nelson Street, Vancouver, B.C., V6G 1M6, Canada
Tel +1 604 730 4059 | Fax +604 730 4059

Bisgrafic www.bisgrafic.com
Avinguda del Mercat 8, 4th Floor, Vic, Barcelona 08500, Spain
Tel +0034 93 883 59 80 | Fax +0034 93 889 55 12

Bleed www.bleed.no
Trondheimsveien 2A, Oslo 0560, Norway
Tel +47 99 30 60 00 | Fax +47 22 20 50 60

BOTH
Helenankatu 4, Helsinki 00170, Finland | Tel +358 40 5846691

bpg
110 S Fairfax Avenue, Suite 355, Los Angeles
CA 90036, United States | Tel 323 954 9522

Brogan & Partners www.brogan.com
325 South Old Woodward, Birmingham, MI 48009, United States
Tel 248 341 8232

Bruketa&Zinic OM www.bruketa-zinic.com
Zavrtnica 17, Zagreb 10 000, Croatia (Local Name: Hrvatska)
Tel +385 1 6064 000 | Fax +385 1 6064 001

Buero Uebele Visuelle Kommunikation www.uebele.com
Heusteugstrasse 94a, Stuttgart 70180, Germany | Tel +49 711 3417020

Carmichael Lynch www.carmichaellynch.com
110 North 5th Street, 10th Floor, Minneapolis, MN 55403
United States | Tel 612 334 6202 | Fax 612 334 6090

Carrió Sánchez Lacasta www.carriosanchezlacasta.com
Infantas, 40 - 5D, Madrid 28004, Spain
Tel +34 914 016 855 | Fax +34 915 218 109

Chris Sanders
150 West 28th Street, #802A, New York, NY 10001, United States
Tel 212 343 0003

Chris van Diemen www.chrisvandiemen.com
Gildestraat 67, Delft, Zuid Holland 2624 AW, Netherlands
Tel +31 6 4192 0279

Cisneros Design Inc. www.cisnerosdesign.com
2904 Rodeo Park Drive East, Suite 200, Santa Fe, NM 87508
United States | Tel 505 471 6699 | Fax 505 438 0436

co:lab www.colabinc.com
56 Arbor Street, Suite 202, Hartford, CT 06106, United States
Tel 860 233 6382

Cold Open www.coldopen.com
1313 Innes Place, Venice, CA 90291, United States
Tel 310 399 3307 | Fax 310 399 3369

Counterform www.counterform.us
10934 SW Celeste Lane, Unit 403, Portland, OR 97225
United States | Tel 503 747 3765

Counterpart Communication Design www.counterpartcd.com
40 South Idlewild, Memphis, TN 38104, United States
Tel 901 323 4900 x104 | Fax 901 578 7878

Cucumber
Skytterveien 12, Bergen, Hordaland NO-5038, Norway
Tel +47 9925 8455 | Fax +47 552 15444

CURIOUS
19a Floral Street, Covent Garden, London WC2E 9DS
United Kingdom | Tel +44 020 7240 6251

Curious Representation
1110 Hubner Avenue, Catonsville, MD 21228, United States
Tel 410 747 0904

David Mellen Design
8111 Bleriot Avenue, Los Angeles, CA 90045, United States
Tel 310 665 0707

David Whitcraft
3543 1/2 Beethoven Street, Los Angeles, CA 90066
United States | Tel 310 497 2076

DDB Los Angeles www.ddbla.com
340 Main Street, Venice, CA 90291, United States
Tel 310 907 1532 | Fax 310 907 1533

EMdash Design
123 Makefield Road, Yardley, PA 19067, United States
Tel 215 932 0548 | Fax 215 337 9192

Eric Chan Design Co. Ltd. www.ericchandesign.com
Unit 601 6F Park Commercial Centre
180 Tung Lo Wan Road Causeway Bay, Hong Kong, Hong Kong
Tel +852 2527 7773 | Fax +852 2865 3929

Fabrique Communications & Design www.fabrique.nl
Oude Delft 201, Delft 2611 HD, Netherlands
Tel +31 15 219 56 00

Faulkner Advertising www.ifaulkner.com
1324 Portesuello Avenue, Santa Barbara, CA 93105-4623
United States | Tel 805 682 0090

Fleishman-Hillard Creative www.creative.fleishmanhillard.com
200 N Broadway, St. Louis, MO 63102, United States
Tel 314 982 9149 | Fax 314 982 9144

Frost Design www.frostdesign.com.au
1st Floor, 15 Foster Street, Surry Hills, Sydney, NSW 2026
Australia | Tel +0061 2 9280 4233 | Fax +0061 2 9280 4266

gggrafik-design www.gggrafik.de
Treitschkestrasse 3, Heidelberg, Baden Wüertemberg 69115
Germany | Tel +49 6221 890 16 56

Goodby, Silverstein & Partners www.gspsf.com
720 California Street, San Francisco, CA 94108, United States
Tel 415 955 5683

Grabarz & Partner Werbeagentur GmbH
Alter Wall 55, Hamburg 20457, Germany
Tel +49 40 37641 0 | Fax + 49 40 37641 400

Graphic Communication Laboratory
311, 5-417-325, Makuhari-Cho, Hanamigwa-ku, Chiba 262-0032
Japan | Tel +81 43 351 5033 | Fax +81 43 351 5033

Great Works www.greatworks.com
530 Broadway, 6th Floor, New York, NY 10012, United States
Tel 646 214 7800

Hiebing www.hiebing.com
315 Wisconsin Avenue, Madison, WI 53703, United States
Tel 608 256 6357 | Fax 608 256 0693

Hitman Corporation
Villa Akasaka 305 Akasaka, Minato-ku, Tokyo 107-0052, Japan
Phone: +81 3 3505 2746 | Fax: +81 3 3505 2782

Hornall Anderson www.hornallanderson.com
710 2nd Avenue, Suite 1300, Seattle, WA 98104, United States
Tel 206 826 2329 | Fax 206 467 6411

Howard, Merrell & Partners www.merrellgroup.com
8521 Six Forks Road, Raleigh, NC 27609, United States
Tel 919 844 2759

HUGTOP Design Company www.hugtop.com.tw
8F, No. 43, Jeng Tai Road, Kaohsiung, Taiwan
Tel +886 7 7116360 | Fax +886 7 7256601

Hyperakt Design Group www.hyperakt.com
401 Smith Street, Brooklyn, NY 11231, United States
Tel 718 855 4250 | Fax 718 855 2754

Jason Dietrick www.jasondietrick.com
3702 N 2nd Street, Harrisburg, PA 17110, United States
Tel 717 557 6683

Jay Advertising www.jayadvertising.com
170 Linden Oaks, Rochester, NY 14625, United States
Tel 585 264 3644

João Machado Design, Lda www.joaomachado.com
Rua Padre Xavier Coutinho, 125 Porto 4150-751, Portugal
Tel +351 226 103 772 | Fax +351 226 103 773

Joaquim Cheong Design
Rua Evora S/N, Edf. Lei Hau 37 Andar E Taipa, Macau, China
Tel +853 2883 5908

Joel Wheat Designs www.joelwheat.com
600 53rd Street S, Birmingham, AL 35212, United States
Tel 205 617 7770 | Fax 205 617 7770

John Rieben Design
330 Pennsylvania Avenue, Ozona, FL 34660, United States
Tel 727 787 9777

Jun Park www.junpark.com
218 Shirley Drive, Richmond Hill, Ontario L4S 1T4, Canada
Tel 905 884 0214

k d geissbühler
Theaterstrasse 10, Ch-8001 Zürich
Tel +0041 44 261 67 61 | Fax +0041 44 261 67 72

Ken-Tsai Lee Design Studio www.kentsailee.com
99-44 62nd Road Rego Park, New York, NY 11374
United States | Tel 171 859 29152

Kimura Design Office,inc.
#504 From-1st. 5-3-10 Minami-Aoyama, Minato-ku, Tokyo 107-0062
Japan | Tel +81 3 3498 7706 | Fax +81 3 3498 7766

KMS TEAM www.kms-team.de
Tölzer Straße 2c, Munich 81379, Germany
Tel +49 89 490411 0

KreativeDept www.kreativedept.com
PO Box 158, Studley, VA 23162, United States
Tel 804 730 1063

Landor Associates
Level 11, 15 Blue Street, North Sydney, New South Wales 2060
Australia | Tel +61 2 8908 8703

Lank Graphic Design & Illustration www.lank.nu
Laxavagen 15, 12844 Bagarmossen, Stockholm 12844
Sweden | Tel +46 8 556 122 22 | Fax +46 8 556 122 21

Lindsay, Stone & Briggs www.lsb.com
100 State Street, Madison, WI 53703-2573, United States
Tel 608 251 7070 | Fax 608 251 8989

Macao Museum of Art www.artmuseum.gov.mo
Rua Evora Edf Flower City Lei Tou, 6 and H, Taipa, Macau | Tel + 853 6628 2990

Mad Studios www.mad-studios.com
2/F, 2C Lau Li Street, Ti Hau, Hong Kong WCH E1, Hong Kong
Tel +852 9414 3291

Malcolm Grear Designers www.mgrear.com
391 Eddy Street, Providence, RI 02903, United States
Tel 401 331 2891 | Fax 401 331 0230

Mark Gowing Design www.markgowing.com
15 Lord Street, Newtown, Sydney, NSW 2016 Australia
Tel +61 2 9517 4871

Marriner Marketing www.marriner.com
10221 Wincopin Circle, Columbia, MD 21044, United States
Tel 410 715 1500

Mehmet Ali Türkmen www.mehmetaliturkmen.com
Cihangir Yokusu, Lale Apartment 8/6, Cihangir, Beyoglu
Istanbul 34433, Turkey | Tel +90 532 292 38 57

Melchior Imboden
Eggertsbühl, Buochs 6374, Switzerland
Tel +004141 6200914 | Fax +004141 6200904

Mende Design www.mendedesign.com
1211 Folsom Street, 4th Floor, San Francisco, CA 94103
United States | Tel 415 431 8200 | Fax 415 431 9695

Michael Schwab Studio www.michaelschwab.com
108 Tamalpais Avenue, San Anselmo, CA 94960, United States
Tel 415 257 5792 | Fax 415 257 5793

Mind Design
James Cookstraat 46-3, Amsterdam 1056 SC, Netherlands
Tel +31 6 15 43 66 96

Mirko Ilic Corp www.mirkoilic.com
207 E 32nd Street, 4th Floor, New York, NY 10016, United States
Tel 212 481 9737 | Fax 212 481 7088

Mono www.mono-1.com
2902 Garfield Avenue S, Minneapolis, MN 55408, United States
Tel 612 822 4135 | Fax 612 822 4136

Naughtyfish design www.naughtyfish.com.au
Suite 306b, 19a Boundary Street, Rushcutters Bay, NSW 2011
Australia | Tel +61 2 9357 5911

NB: Studio www.nbstudio.co.uk
4-8 Emerson Street, London SE1 9DU, United Kingdom
Tel +44 0 20 7633 9046 | Fax +44 0 20 3267 1019

Niklaus Troxler Design www.troxlerart.ch
Bahnhofstrasse 22, Postfach, Willisau CH-6130, Switzerland
Tel +41 41 970 2731 | Fax +41 41 970 3231

omdr design agency www.omdr.co.jp
#202, 6-12-10, Minamiaoyama Minato-ku, Tokyo, Japan
Tel +81 3 5766 3410 | Fax +81 3 5766 3411

One Hundred Church Street
100 Church Street, Logan, UT 84321-4621, United States
Tel 435 753 0593 | Fax 435 753 0593

Optima Soulsight USA www.optimasoulsight.com
1899 2nd Street, Highland Park, IL 60035, United States
Tel 847 681 4444 | Fax 847 681 4445

Original Loiri Oy www.originalloiri.fi
Selkamerenk, 7 C 43, Helsinki 00180, Finland | Tel +358 9 685 2854

Palio www.palio.com
260 Broadway, Saratoga Springs, NY 12866, United States
Tel 518 226 4126 | Fax 518 583 1560

Paone Design Associates www.paonedesign.com
240 South Twentieth Street, Third Floor, Philadelphia, PA 19103-5602
United States | Tel 215 893 0144 | Fax 215 893 0261

Pentagram Design, Austin www.pentagram.com
1508 West Fifth Street, Austin, TX 78703, United States
Tel 512 476 3076 | Fax 512 476 5725

Pentagram Design, New York www.pentagram.com
204 Fifth Avenue, New York, NY 10010, United States
Tel 212 802 0261 | Fax 212 532 0181

Pentagram Design, Berlin www.pentagram.com
Leibnizstrasse 60, Berlin 10629, Germany
Tel +49 30 27 87 610 | Fax +49 30 27 87 61 10

Pirtle Design Inc. www.pirtledesign.com
89 Church Hill Road, New Paltz, NY 12561, United States
Tel 845 658 3908

Piscatello Design Centre www.piscatello.com
330 West 38th Street Suite 1005, New York, NY 10018
United States | Tel 212 502 4734

Punktum Design MDD www.punktumdesign.dk
Pakhus 12, Dampfaergevej 8-5th floor, Copenhagen, DK 2100
Denmark | Tel +45 20320063

Range
2257 Vantage Street, Dallas, TX 75207, United States
Tel 214 744 0555

Rebeca Mendez Design www.rebecamendez.com
11009 1/2 Strathmore Drive, Los Angeles, CA 90024, United States
Tel 310 985 0621

Rose Design www.rosedesign.co.uk
The Old School, 70 St. Marychurch Street, London SE16 4HZ
United Kingdom | Tel +44 0 20 7394 2800

Ryan Russell Design
195 Brynwood Drive, Port Matilda, PA 16870, United States
Tel 814 880 6377

Sagmeister, Inc. www.sagmeister.com
222 W 14 Street, New York, NY 10011, United States
Tel 212 647 1789

Saint Hieronymus Press www.goines.net
1703 Martin Luther King, Jr. Way, Berkeley, CA 94709
United States | Tel 510 549 1405

San Francisco Museum of Modern Art www.sfmoma.org
151 Third Street, San Francisco, CA 94103, United States
Tel 415 357 4110

Scorsone/Drueding: SDPOSTERS.COM www.sdposters.com
212 Greenwood Avenue, Jenkintown, PA 19046, United States
Tel 215 572 0782

Sean Kennedy Santos Fotografie www.sksantos.net
244 Madison Ave, Suite 3640, New York, NY 10016
United States | Phone: 212 679 2172 | Fax: 212 679 1024

Shin Matsunaga Design Inc.
Shinjuku-ku, Yarai-cho, 98-4, Tokyo 162-0805, Japan
Tel +81 3 5225 0777 | Fax +81 3 3266 5600

Sibley/Peteet Design www.spdaustin.com
522 East 6th Street, Austin, TX 78701, United States
Tel 512 473 2333

Siquis www.siquis.com
1340 Smith Avenue, Suite 300, Baltimore, MD 21209
United States | Tel 410 323 4800

Skolos-Wedell www.skolos-wedell.com
125 Green Street, Canton, MA 02021, United States
Tel 781 828 0280

Staccato www.staccatodesign.com
1930 NE 201st Avenue, Fairview, OR 97024, United States
Tel 503 827 0933

stereo-type
4F, 317-1, Star-Building, Sangsu-dong, Mapo-gu
Seoul 121-829, South Korea | Tel +82 10 3434 3991

Studio International www.studio-international.com
Buconjiceva 43, Zagreb HR-10 000
Croatia (local Name: Hrvatska)
Tel +385 1 37 40 404 | Fax +385 1 37 08 320

Studio Joseph Jibri www.josephjibri.com
20 Wissotzky Street, Tel Aviv 62338, Israel
Tel +972 3 6850037 | Fax +972 3 5443614

Studio Uwe Loesch
Mettmanner Strasse 25, Erkrath 40699, Germany
Tel +49 211 55 848

SVI Design www.svidesign.com
Westbourne Studio 126, 242 Acklam Road, London W10 5JJ
United Kingdom | Tel +44 020 7524 7808 | Fax +44 793 213 6333

Taber Calderon www.tabercalderon.com
414 E 120th Street, New York, NY 10035, United States
Tel 917 282 7742

Takashi Akiyama www.tamabi.ac.jp/gurafu/akiyama/
3-14-35 Shimo-Ochiai Shinjuku-ku, Tokyo 161-0033, Japan
Tel +81 3 3565 4316 | Fax +81 3 5996 9376

Taku Satoh Design Office Inc. www.tsdo.jp
Ginsho bldg. 4F, 1-14-11 Ginza, Chuo-ku, Tokyo 104-0061
Japan | Tel +81 3 3538 2051

tbd advertising www.tbdadvertising.com
856 NW Bond Street, Suite 2, Bend, OR 97701, United States
Tel 541 388 7558 | Fax 541 388 7532

TeamDesign
P.O. Box #4, Moscow 117648, Russian Federation
Tel +7 495 987 4347

Texas State University - San Marcos www.txstate.edu
7253 Mt. Sharp Road, Wimberley, TX 78676, United States
Tel 512 245 2611

The Martin Agency www.martinagency.com
One Shockoe Plaza, Richmond, VA 23219, United States
Tel 804 698 8750 | Fax 804 698 8722

The Partners www.thepartners.co.uk
Albion Courtyard, Greenhill Rents, Smithfield, London EC1M 6PQ
United Kingdom | Tel +44 20 7689 4618

Thonik www.thonik.nl
Weespezijde 79D, Amsterdam 1091 EJ, Netherlands
Tel +31 20 468 3525 | Fax +31 20 468 3524

TOKY Branding + Design www.toky.com
3001 Locust Street, St. Louis, MO 63103, United States
Tel 314 534 2000 | Fax 314 534 2001

Toyotsugu Itoh Design Office
402 Royal Villa Tsurumai, 4-17-8 Tsurumai, Showa-ku, Nagoya
Aichi Prefecture 466-0064, Japan
Tel +81 52 731 9747

University of Wisconsin - Green Bay www.uwgb.edu
P.O. Box 142, New Franken, WI 54229, United States
Tel 920 465 5147

Vanderbyl Design www.vanderbyldesign.com
171 2nd Street, 2nd Floor, San Francisco, CA 94105
United States | Tel 415 543 8447 | Fax 415 543 9058

Vision Creative Inc. www.visioncreativeinc.com
10619-102 Avenue, Edmonton, Alberta T5J 2Z3, Canada
Tel +780 452 3434 | Fax +780 455 4567

Visual Arts Press, Ltd. www.schoolofvisualarts.edu
220 East 23rd Street, Suite 311, New York, NY 10010
United States | Tel +212 592 2380 | Fax 212 696 0552

visuelle kommunikation
Barbarastrass 8, Bergheim, Nordrhein-westfalen 50129
Germany | Tel +49 177 2348182

VSA Partners, Inc. www.vsapartners.com
1347 South State Street, Chicago, IL 60605, United States
Phone 212 869 1188, 312 427 6413 | Fax 312 869 0099

WAX www.waxpartnership.com
320 333 24th Avenue SW, Calgary T2S 3E6, Canada | Tel 403 262 9323

WONGDOODY www.wongdoody.com
1011 Western Avenue, Suite 900, Seattle, WA 98104, United States
Tel 206 624 5325 | Fax 206 624 2369

CreativeStrategists

DesignDirectors

Designers

PrintProducers

ProjectManagers

Typographers

DesignFirms

Clients

Two ways to dramatically save on our Books!

Graphis Design Titles

Poster Annual 2010

Design Annual 2010

New Talent Annual 2009

Advertising 2009

Annual Reports 2009

Brochures 6

Letterhead 7

Logo 7

Product Design 3

Promotion Design 2

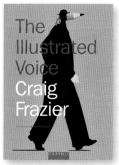

The Illustrated Voice

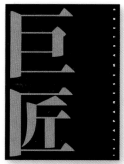

12 Japanese Masters

designing:
Chermayeff & Geismar

Exhibition:
The Work of Socio X

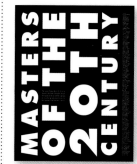

Masters 20th Century

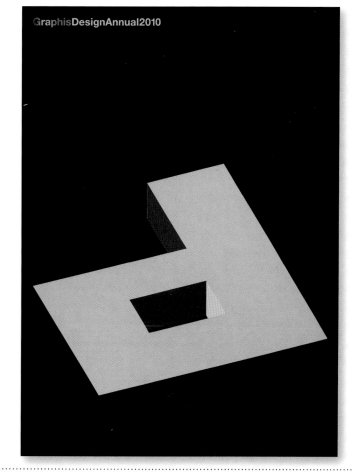